Money Wisdom

The Laws That Govern Wealth

DK GLOBAL PUBLICATIONS

Money Wisdom

The Laws That Govern Wealth

Dr David Kaluba

www.davidkaluba.com

Money Wisdom

⚭ The Laws That Govern Wealth

By Dr David Kaluba

Published by DK Global Publishing

London, United Kingdom

All rights reserved ©DK Global Limited

ISBN: 9798884277960

Copyright ©2024 by DK Global Publishing

Published in the United Kingdom

"Your biggest problem is not a lack of money, but a lack of success ideas."

"Wealth creation is not a secret reserved for only a select few, anyone willing to learn and act can achieve untold riches in this lifetime."

@davidkaluba

DEDICATION

I Am overjoyed and humbled to have the privilege of placing this precious book in your hands. With much love, I dedicate this book to my priceless family and friends, who are not only a source of inspiration for me but are great encouragement and pillars for perseverance in the hardest of times. There is no greater fulfilment in this life than to spend time with loved ones and to share your success and accomplishments with those who do life with you. I am incredibly grateful for the privilege to enjoy meaningful relationships with you my precious family and friends. I gladly dedicate this book to you all, I love you all dearly and deeply appreciate each one of you. I look forward to celebrating many victories with you as we win together in this amazing journey of life. And remember, that you are an integral part in this grand spectacle that is life, and you have what it takes to win big in this generation. May you prosper beyond your wildest dreams as you enjoy the contents of this book: "Money Wisdom and the Keys that Govern Wealth."

TABLE OF CONTENTS

1. Forward By Mark Polack — 8
2. Introduction – Conceive it, believe it, achieve it — 11
3. Neuroplasticity: See Yourself Wealthy — 15
4. Delayed Gratification — 19
5. Be the Solution — 22
6. Wealth is not an accident — 25
7. Time: The most precious capital — 32
8. Financial Independence — 38
9. The Laws that Govern Money — 44
10. The Law of Supply and Demand — 51
11. The Law of Compounding — 54
12. The Law of Risk and Reward — 58
13. The Law of Scarcity — 62
14. The Law of Value Creation — 65
15. Making Money vs Earning Money — 69
16. The Law of Attraction — 74
17. The Emergency (Crisis) Fund — 78
18. Living within your means — 81
19. Using Money as your servant — 84
20. The Law of Direction — 87
21. The Law of Association — 90
22. The Law of Leverage — 94
23. The Law of Seasons — 98
24. The Law of Diversification — 102
25. Money can Make or Break you — 106
26. Money is an Amplifier — 109
27. Money does not like stagnancy — 113
28. Build the life you want — 117

29.	The Power of Passive Income	123
30.	Money Does not Segregate	129
31.	Assets vs Liabilities	133
32.	Bad Debt vs Good Debt	137
33.	Let us talk about Credit Cards	141
34.	Repairing your Credit Score	147
35.	Learn Simple Budgeting	160
36.	Defeat the Poverty Mindset	165
37.	Money answers all things	169
38.	The Power of Self-Development	175
39.	Have a Financial Plan	183
40.	The Wealth Formula	192
41.	How the Rich get richer, and the Poor get poorer	200
42.	The Mindset of Successful People	207
43.	Get out of the Rat Race	216
44.	Successful Goal setting	224
45.	The Art of Prioritising	234
46.	Be Coachable	240
47.	Understanding the Language of Wealth and Money	246
48.	Understanding Investments	259
49.	Understanding Savings	268
50.	The Power of Authenticity	272
51.	The Power of Focus	276
52.	The Art of Consistency	282
53.	The Power of Adaptability	287
54.	SWOT Analysis	291
55.	Transformational Thinking	295
56.	My Concluding Thoughts	300

FORWARD

BY MARK POLACK

FORWARD BY MARK POLACK

It is with immense pleasure and enthusiasm that I pen this foreword for "Money Wisdom and the Laws That Govern Wealth," authored by the esteemed Dr David Kaluba. I have known Dr David for many years. I am an entrepreneur with over 40 years of business experience covering industries as diverse as fashion, telecommunications, finance and health. I have been involved with growing and developing businesses at a local, national and international level and employed my skills to implement business systems to generate profit for these companies. Over the years, my relationship with Dr Kaluba continues to grow as I have seen him apply these laws which I now use in my own business pursuits. David has the rare ability to understand these Laws that Govern Wealth and be able to apply them to great effect gaining positive outcomes in different businesses, industries and countries. These laws are not theories, so when applied to real life financial situations the results are as sure as the law of gravity. As an accomplished entrepreneur, a certified success coach, a thoughtful leader, and prolific author of several best-selling books, and a close friend of mine, Dr Kaluba brings a wealth of knowledge, experience, and insight to the realm of financial literacy and wealth creation. In today's fast-paced and ever-changing world, the pursuit of financial success and abundance has become a cornerstone of modern life. However, amidst the myriad of financial advice and strategies available, itis rare to find a comprehensive and insightful guide that not only illuminates the principles of wealth creation but also deals with the underlying laws and universal truths that govern our financial destinies. In "Money Wisdom," Dr Kaluba masterfully navigates the intricate web of financial concepts, principles, and practices, offering readers a roadmap to financial independence and prosperity. Drawing upon his experience as an entrepreneur, a founding director, and his deep understanding of economic principles, he distils complex financial concepts into clear, actionable insights that readers can apply to their own lives. What sets "Money Wisdom" apart is Dr Kaluba's unique ability to blend practical wisdom with timeless principles. Through engaging anecdotes, real-life examples, and thought-provoking exercises, he empowers readers to challenge their limiting beliefs, embrace abundance mindset, and harness the laws that govern wealth to create a life of purpose and prosperity. As you embark on this enlightening journey through the pages of "Money Wisdom," I encourage you to approach the material with an open mind and a willingness to challenge conventional wisdom. Dr Kaluba's profound insights and practical wisdom will inspire you to take bold action, make informed financial decisions, and unlock the full potential of your financial future. In closing, I extend my heartfelt gratitude to Dr David Kaluba for sharing his wisdom, expertise, and passion for financial empowerment with readers around the world. "Money Wisdom" is a testament to his commitment to excellence, his passion for people and his unwavering dedication to helping others achieve financial success and abundance.

With deepest respect and admiration,

JM Polack

Mark Polack - CEO of Smart Organic Solutions (SOS)

8th March 2024

CONCEIVE IT

BELIEVE IT

ACHIEVE IT

2. INTRODUCTION: CONCEIVE IT, BELIEVE IT, ACHIEVE IT!

"Money Wisdom and The Laws That Govern Wealth" encapsulates the essence of harnessing financial empowerment through the power of mindset and action. This philosophy emphasises three fundamental principles: conception, belief, and achievement. There is no better place for me to start authoring this book than right here you're your beliefs and philosophy. I have chosen to call my introduction, "conceive it, believe it, achieve it" because your intrinsic character is critical to your financial success, and every area of your life.

Firstly, conception involves envisioning one's financial goals and aspirations with clarity and purpose. By articulating an unclouded vision of what financial success looks like, you can create a roadmap to guide your actions and decisions.

Secondly, belief plays a pivotal role in the journey towards financial empowerment. It involves cultivating a mindset of abundance, self-confidence, and positivity. Believing in your ability to attain financial goals is essential for overcoming challenges and setbacks along the way.

The resulting achievement is the culmination of consistent effort, perseverance, and determination. By taking focused action aligned with your financial vision and maintaining unwavering belief in your ability to succeed, you can turn your financial aspirations into tangible reality.

"Money Wisdom" serves as a guiding philosophy for individuals seeking to unlock their full potential for financial success and abundance. By embracing these key principles, you can cultivate a mindset of empowerment and take proactive steps towards realising your financial dreams.

In a world where financial prosperity seems both elusive and essential, the pursuit of wealth often feels like an enigma wrapped in a mystery. Countless individuals embark on this journey, armed with ambition and determination, only to find themselves lost in a labyrinth of financial decisions and uncertainties. Yet, amidst the chaos, there exists a select group who navigate the realms of wealth with effortless grace and clarity, those who possess the elusive quality known as "money wisdom," those who understand the laws that govern wealth.

In "Money Wisdom and The Keys That Govern Wealth," we embark on a transformative exploration into the principles that underpin financial success. Through the pages of this book, we delve deep into the realms of wealth, unlocking the secrets that separate the financially empowered from the financially constrained.

Drawing upon centuries of collective wisdom and contemporary insights, "Money Wisdom" serves as a beacon of guidance in a sea of financial noise. We uncover the fundamental truths that govern the accumulation, preservation, and growth of wealth, providing readers with a roadmap to navigate their own financial journey with confidence and purpose.

From the psychology of money to the mechanics of investments, from the importance of financial literacy to the power of mindset, each chapter of "Money Wisdom" offers invaluable insights and practical strategies to empower readers to take control of their financial destinies.

But "Money Wisdom" is more than just a guide to financial success – it is a manifesto for a change in basic assumptions in our relationship with wealth. It challenges conventional notions of prosperity and invites readers to redefine their understanding of abundance, not merely as a measure of material possessions, but as a reflection of holistic well-being.

As we embark on this transformative journey together, let us heed the wisdom of the ages and the lessons of modernity. Let us transcend the confines of financial scarcity and embrace a new paradigm of abundance. Let us unlock the keys that govern wealth and embark on a journey towards financial freedom, fulfilment, and true prosperity. Welcome to "Money Wisdom," a comprehensive guide designed to empower you with the knowledge and tools to achieve financial success and abundance. In this book, we will embark on a transformative journey together, exploring the principles and practices that govern wealth and prosperity.

NEUROPLASTICITY:

WHAT DO YOU SEE?

3. NEUROPLASTICITY: WHAT DO YOU SEE?

Neuroplasticity, the brain's remarkable ability to reorganize itself by forming new neural connections throughout life, has profound implications for wealth creation. In this chapter, we delve into the meaning of neuroplasticity and explore how understanding and harnessing this phenomenon can empower you to create wealth and financial abundance, a life of choice and lasting freedom.

Understanding Neuroplasticity: Neuroplasticity, also known as brain plasticity, refers to the brain's capacity to adapt, change, and rewire itself in response to experiences, behaviours, and environmental stimuli. Contrary to the long-held belief that the brain's structure is fixed, research has shown that the brain is incredibly malleable and capable of remodelling its neural networks in response to learning, practice, and various life experiences, including damage and severe injury.

Neuroplasticity plays a pivotal role in shaping individuals' attitudes, behaviours, and beliefs related to wealth creation. By understanding and harnessing the power of neuroplasticity, individuals can rewire their brains to adopt a mindset of abundance, cultivate positive money habits, and pursue opportunities for financial growth and success. Here are some keys that will help you get on your way to transformation your mind and the way think and respond to wealth and money:

Rewire the limiting beliefs in your life. Neuroplasticity offers a pathway for you to challenge and reframe limiting beliefs about money and wealth. By consciously engaging in positive affirmations, visualisation techniques, and cognitive restructuring exercises, individuals can reshape your neural pathways to align with beliefs that support wealth creation. Over time, these new neural connections reinforce a mindset of abundance and possibility, enabling you to overcome self-imposed limitations and pursue your financial goals with confidence. To transform your fortunes, your mind must change first, and this is your greatest superpower.

Cultivate financial literacy and never stop learning otherwise you will either become redundant or a relic. Neuroplasticity facilitates the acquisition and retention of financial knowledge and skills. Through continuous learning, practice, and exposure to innovative ideas, you can strengthen the neural connections associated with financial literacy and decision-making. By engaging in activities such as reading financial literature, attending workshops, and seeking mentorship, you can enhance your understanding of wealth creation strategies and make informed financial choices that align with your goals.

Develop resilience and grit using the power of your mind. Neuroplasticity enables you to cultivate resilience, perseverance, and grit in the face of financial challenges and setbacks. By intentionally exposing yourself to discomfort and adversity, you can strengthen the neural circuits associated with resilience and emotional regulation. As a result, you will become better equipped to navigate obstacles, bounce back from setbacks, and stay focused on your long-term financial goals and objectives.

Seize opportunities for growth by instructing your way of things and perception. Neuroplasticity empowers you to embrace opportunities for growth and innovation in the pursuit of wealth creation. By fostering a growth mindset characterised by curiosity, creativity, and adaptability, you can expand your neural networks and open yourself up to new possibilities. Whether it involves exploring entrepreneurial ventures, investing in new markets, or pursuing unconventional career paths, neuroplasticity enables you to embrace change, take calculated risks, and capitalise on opportunities for financial success.

Neuroplasticity is a powerful tool that you can leverage to create wealth and financial abundance. By understanding the brain's capacity for change and adaptation, you can rewire your neural networks to adopt a mindset of abundance, cultivate positive money habits, and pursue opportunities for growth and success. As we continue to unlock the mysteries of the brain, harnessing the power of neuroplasticity will play an increasingly vital role in shaping the future of wealth creation and financial empowerment. As powerful and sophisticated as your brain is, your brain does not have the ability to distinguish between reality and imagination. Your brain takes instructions from your mind and whatever you strongly focus on, will instruct your brain, which then informs how you respond and behave.

DELAYED GRATIFICATION

4. DELAYED GRATIFICATION

In today's world of instant gratification and consumerism, the concept of delaying immediate rewards for long-term gains may seem counterintuitive. However, the ability to practice delayed gratification is a cornerstone principle in wealth creation and financial wisdom. In this chapter, we will explore the profound impact of delayed gratification on building wealth, making prudent financial decisions, and cultivating a mindset of abundance. Delayed gratification refers to the ability to resist the temptation of immediate rewards in favour of larger, more significant rewards in the future. This principle involves making sacrifices and exhibiting self-discipline in the short term to achieve greater benefits over time. While it may require patience and perseverance, delayed gratification is a powerful tool for achieving long-term financial success.

One of the primary ways delayed gratifications contributes to wealth creation is by fostering disciplined saving and investment habits. Instead of spending impulsively on discretionary items, individuals who practice delayed gratification allocate their resources towards savings, investments, and assets that generate long-term returns. By prioritizing long-term financial goals over short-term indulgences, they lay the foundation for sustainable wealth accumulation. Your willingness to wait will make you rich.

Moreover, delayed gratification plays a crucial role in avoiding debt and maintaining financial stability. Individuals who resist the temptation to overspend on credit and consumer debt are better positioned to build a strong financial foundation and avoid the burden of high-interest payments. By living within their means and prioritising saving over spending, you will establish a solid financial footing that will enable them to pursue wealth-building opportunities and see you achieve all your financial goals.

In addition to its impact on saving and investing, delayed gratification influences various aspects of financial decision-making. It encourages you to carefully evaluate your options, weigh the potential risks and rewards, and prioritise your long-term financial well-being. Whether it involves choosing between immediate consumption and long-term investment or deferring discretionary expenses for future financial goals, practicing delayed gratification empowers you to make prudent financial decisions aligned with your objectives.

Delayed gratification will help you cultivate a Mindset of Abundance, and will have a tangible impact on wealth creation, as it contributes to the development of a mindset of abundance and financial empowerment. By recognising the value of patience, discipline, and delayed rewards, you shift your focus from immediate desires to long-term aspirations. This shift in perspective fosters a sense of confidence, resilience, and optimism about the future, enabling you to navigate financial challenges with grace and determination.

The power of delayed gratification cannot be overstated in the context of wealth creation and financial wisdom. By embracing this principle, you can cultivate disciplined saving and investing habits, make prudent financial decisions, and foster a mindset of abundance. While it may require sacrifice and self-discipline in the short term, the long-term benefits of delayed gratification are undeniable, paving the way for sustainable wealth accumulation and financial empowerment.

BE THE SOLUTION

5. BE THE SOLUTION

Instead of complaining about the state of the world and everything around you, this book will equip you to be the solution and the answer that your family, your business and your community have been waiting for. In a world filled with challenges and opportunities, you have the power to become the solution by leveraging your financial resources and cultivating money wisdom. In this chapter, we explore how creating wealth and embracing money wisdom can empower you to make a positive impact in your life and your community.

Wealth creation is not merely about accumulating material possessions but about gaining the resources and autonomy to effect positive change. By generating wealth through entrepreneurship, investments, and innovation, you can empower yourself to address societal challenges, pursue your passions, and make meaningful contributions to the world.

Entrepreneurship offers a powerful platform for you to become the solution by creating value, driving innovation, and addressing unmet needs in society. By launching businesses that solve pressing problems, as an entrepreneur, you can generate wealth while making a positive impact on your community. Whether it involves developing sustainable solutions to environmental issues, providing access to essential services, or fostering economic empowerment, entrepreneurship enables you to become an agent of change and a catalyst for social progress.

Investing in social impact ventures and initiatives is another avenue through which you can become the solution. By allocating capital towards businesses and organizations that prioritise social and environmental objectives, investors can leverage their financial resources to drive positive change. Impact investing, philanthropy, and socially responsible investing strategies will enable you to support causes aligned with your values while generating financial returns that contribute to your wealth and well-being. Be the change that you wish to see by taking the lead.

Money wisdom goes beyond financial literacy and wealth accumulation; it encompasses a holistic understanding of how to leverage resources responsibly and ethically to create lasting positive outcomes. By cultivating money wisdom, you can maximise the impact of your wealth creation efforts and ensure sustainable prosperity for yourself and future generations.

Money wisdom involves mindful spending habits that align with personal values and long-term goals. By prioritising purchases that contribute to well-being, sustainability, and social good, you can make a positive impact through your consumer choices. Conscious consumption encourages you to support businesses and products that promote ethical practices, environmental stewardship, and social responsibility.

Financial literacy is a cornerstone of money wisdom, enabling you to make informed decisions about money management, investing, and wealth building. By educating yourself and others about personal finance principles and strategies, you can empower yourself and your community to achieve financial independence and security.

Becoming the solution through wealth creation and money wisdom is not only a pathway to personal prosperity but also a means of creating positive change in the world. By leveraging your financial resources and cultivating a mindset of abundance and responsibility, you can empower yourself to address pressing challenges, support meaningful causes, and leave a legacy of impact and prosperity. You can truly make an indelible mark on your generation and on many generations to come, long after you are no longer of this world. This is one of my greatest motivations for writing this book. My desire is to empower as many people as are willing to get understanding to practice these proven keys for success and wealth creation. As we embrace the power of money wisdom, we can collectively shape a future where financial empowerment and social progress go hand in hand.

WEALTH CREATION IS NOT AN ACCIDENT

6. WEALTH CREATION IS NOT AN ACCIDENT

Wealth creation is often perceived as a stroke of luck or an accidental occurrence reserved for the fortunate few. However, upon closer examination, it becomes evident that wealth is not the result of happenstance but rather the product of intentional design, disciplined action, and strategic planning. In this chapter, we explore the notion that wealth creation is a deliberate endeavour that requires focus, effort, and a commitment to financial empowerment.

Contrary to widely held belief, wealth creation is not solely determined by external factors such as inheritance or luck. While external circumstances may play a role, true wealth creation is rooted in intentional actions and decisions that align with long-term financial goals and aspirations. By adopting a proactive mindset and taking deliberate steps towards financial empowerment, you can create opportunities for wealth accumulation and abundance.

Wealth creation begins with setting clear, specific, and achievable financial goals. Whether it involves saving for retirement, starting a business, or investing in real estate, defining concrete objectives provides a roadmap for wealth creation and guides decision-making processes. By articulating your financial aspirations and establishing actionable goals, you can create a framework for intentional wealth creation.

Develop a strategic plan because intentional wealth creation requires a strategic approach that encompasses saving, investing, and asset allocation strategies. By developing a comprehensive financial plan tailored to your unique circumstances and objectives, you can optimize their resources and maximise opportunities for wealth accumulation. Strategic planning involves assessing risk tolerance, diversifying investments, and adjusting strategies as needed to adapt to changing economic conditions. And the world around you is always changing.

Cultivate positive money habits, as nothing just happens in life. Wealth creation is sustained by cultivating positive money habits that support long-term financial growth and stability. This includes practices such as budgeting, saving consistently, and living within or below your means. By prioritizing financial discipline and avoiding impulsive spending, you can build a solid foundation for wealth creation and mitigate financial risks.

Invest in personal and professional development. Intentional wealth creation involves investing in oneself through continuous learning, skill development, and personal growth. By enhancing your knowledge, expertise, and capabilities, you can increase your earning potential and create opportunities for career advancement or entrepreneurial ventures. Investing in education, training, and professional networking fosters a mindset of growth and positions you for long-term financial success. Most people say education is expensive, but you will soon discover that ignorance costs so much more.

Leverage opportunities and resources because wealth creation requires a proactive approach to identifying and leveraging opportunities for financial growth. This may involve exploring new income streams, capitalising on market trends, or leveraging financial resources such as loans or investments. By staying informed, adaptable, and resourceful, you can seize opportunities for wealth creation and capitalize on favourable economic conditions.

Wealth creation is not a matter of chance or luck but rather a deliberate and intentional process that requires focus, effort, and a commitment to financial empowerment. By setting clear goals, developing strategic plans, cultivating positive money habits, investing in personal development, and leveraging opportunities, you can design your path to wealth and create a legacy of prosperity for yourself and future generations. Wealth creation is within reach for those who are willing to take intentional steps towards financial empowerment and abundance.

Nothing just happens and reaping is always reserved for the planters, so if you are not reaping, it is very possible that you never put any seed in the ground. And if you did sow but you do not like your harvest, then you need to check your seed. A law is a universal principle that defines the fundamental nature of an entity and applies to everyone without segregation such as the law of gravity. This is a law and cannot be changed whether you like it or not so if you do not like your harvest, change your seed and if you do not like the seed, change the Sower, which is you by the way; change yourself and become better instead of blaming everyone around you. In the same way, do not go around looking for excuses and reasons why you have not succeeded or why things will not work but rather focus on improving yourself and sharpening your skills.

The three main laws that govern sowing and reaping are that you cannot escape the consequences of one's actions, you reap more than you sow, and you reap much later than what you sow. You cannot sow anything and just pray, but expect a harvest, which is just not wise. But it is obvious that it makes no sense for a farmer to sit down in front of his field with a basket waiting for a harvest when he put nothing in the ground or for him to go into the field looking for apples when he only sowed corn in his field. The harvest will always look like the seed and will be more.

There are many ways to sow so there is no need to bring anyone down or compete with anyone out there. Only you can do what you were born to do and if you stick to your own lane, you absolutely have no competition. The world has enough resources for everyone to make it in life and become extraordinarily successful. No one should ever fear that the 'success cake' will run out if somebody else succeeds, instead create your own seed, find your own soil and you will reap your own harvest.

Sometimes you will win and sometimes you will lose, this law is both positive and negative. You must understand that failure is a part of winning in life for every victory carries scars of past failures. As you sow your seed, sometimes you will reap a good harvest but sometimes you will drop some revenue. Understanding this concept will save you a lot of unnecessary tears and disappointment as you learn how to deal with the down times of life and business. Some of the greatest lessons I have ever picked up in life came through the most challenging times of my life. And at the time, I never thought I would make it, but I am still here because all things work for my good.

The law of sowing and reaping will work for anyone regardless of background, race, colour, or nationality. Just because you do not believe in the law of gravity does not mean that if you jump off a 9-story building with no parachute, gravity will not take you down. It is a law, and it demands that you obey it, therefore, you are going down. When you do nothing and do not sow, you are guaranteed to lose! The only time you lose in life is when you refuse to act and do nothing. It is the same principle that applies to quitting. But if you apply yourself, you will certainly get feedback whether good or bad. I would much rather try and fail rather than not try at all.

Seasons will come and go and there is nothing you can do about it but understanding them gives you the advantage. There are things that will happen outside of your control such as global recessions, inflation, the political climate, natural disasters etc. Staying on top is all about leveraging the tough times by using them to your advantage and making the most of the favourable seasons. There is a season for everything in life, for example, a season for driving an extremely fast car with a huge tank and extremely high insurance and a season to stick to a minimal maintenance vehicle that agrees with your current cashflow. Whatever you do and whatever happens, keep on sowing just like the Sower in the story did. When you quit for whatever reason, you are out of the game and have already lost but if you hang in there and ride out the storm, it is only a matter of time before the markets, and you recover. Broken focus is one of the main reasons for most failures in business, stay focused and stick to your lane. Discipline your disappointment and refuse to quit when the going gets tough. It is the last man standing who takes the crown home. Whether good or bad, harvest will always come, the only question is what type of harvest you are looking for. To try and prevent a harvest from our words and actions is like trying to stop the sun from coming out in the morning. This certainty is a wonderful thing if you are putting good seed in the ground because then you know that it is only a matter of time before you are standing the middle of your vision.

TIME: THE MOST PRECIOUS CAPITAL

7. TIME: THE MOST PRECIOUS CAPITAL

In the pursuit of wealth creation, we often focus on financial resources, investment strategies, and business acumen. However, amidst the complexities of wealth accumulation, we often overlook our most precious and finite asset: time. In this chapter, we delve into the significance of time as our most valuable capital for wealth creation and explore how maximizing its potential can lead to long-term financial prosperity.

The Value of Time in Wealth Creation cannot be overstated, as it is the most critical element that underpins your journey to success. Time is a unique and irreplaceable resource that plays a pivotal role in wealth creation. Unlike money, which can be earned and spent, time is finite and cannot be reclaimed once it has passed. Understanding the value of time is essential for individuals seeking to build wealth and achieve financial freedom.

Time is a critical factor in the phenomenon of compound interest for example, and Albert Einstein famously referred to it as the "eighth wonder of the world." Compound interest allows investments to grow exponentially over time, as earnings generate additional earnings. The longer the time horizon, the greater the impact of compound interest on wealth accumulation. By starting early and allowing investments to compound over time, you can harness the power of time to build substantial wealth and financial success.

The importance of long-term thinking therefore comes into play. Wealth creation requires a mindset of long-term thinking and patience. While it may be tempting to seek quick returns or engage in speculative investments, sustainable wealth is often built through consistent, long-term strategies. By adopting a patient approach and focusing on investments with proven records and growth potential, you can capitalise on the compounding effect of time and achieve lasting financial success.

Learn to leverage time for skill development and education. Time is invaluable for personal and professional development, which is essential for wealth creation. Investing time in acquiring new skills, expanding knowledge, and pursuing educational opportunities can enhance earning potential and open doors to new career opportunities or entrepreneurial ventures. Continuous learning and skill development enable you to adapt to changing market conditions, innovate, and capitalise on emerging trends in wealth creation.

Time is a catalyst for entrepreneurship and innovation for aspiring entrepreneurs. It is a critical factor in the journey of building successful businesses. Starting early allows entrepreneurs to experiment, iterate, and learn from failures, increasing the likelihood of success. Additionally, time provides you with the opportunity to build valuable networks, establish credibility, and develop expertise in your respective industries. By leveraging time effectively, you can bring innovative ideas to fruition, create value for customers, and generate wealth through entrepreneurial ventures.

All of life can be summed up as time, but life is full of experiences and their intensity which are accumulated over time. However, we all have a limited supply so make today count and understand the power of now! We have all been given the dignity of having choice as human beings. Apart from working hard, working smarter is just as important. Every time you embark on a project, it will either run your life or you will run the project, so take charge of the moving parts and make sure it all fits in to give you the best quality of life. Everyone has the same 24 hours in a day to achieve goals and objectives. It is not the hours that you put in that count, but what you do with your hours, which is why the same 24 hours will produce a millionaire while others remain broke. Identify the important things of life, prioritise your meetings, your phone calls, your visits and even your social life. You end up wasting so much valuable time when you have no agenda for your life and just randomly involve yourself in various commitments.

Please do not mistake doing things for productivity, movement is not necessarily achievement until the deal is signed and sealed. Do your best to deliberately separate your time into specific categories as it is the only way you can live in the moment. If you are on business, focus on the business and be in the moment, if you are working, focus on the work and be in that moment. In the same way, when it is time for family quality time, make sure that you give yourself and your family the best you in that moment. If you spend your life thinking of other things while doing something else, you will never fully give yourself to any one thing and hence will never fully be maximised.

Cut out time-wasting habits and activities because your time is the most important capital that you have. It is even more precious than money. Guard your time like you would guard a million pounds because your time can give you multiple millions when you respect it. Write things down if you must and make sure that you follow through. Write it all down and run with it, put in where you can see it, have a game plan, a vision board or whatever helps you see where you are going. This way, you not only know exactly what you are doing and where you are going but it will also help keep you focused and stick to your lane. Get an organised journal whether electronic or a traditional paper one so that you can always refer to it every now and then.

One of the greatest enemies of your time is putting things off for later; please remember that procrastination is not your friend! Get in the habit of acting now if you want to get ahead in life. The grave is full of dreams that where never fulfilled because the people who carried them were waiting for the right time, for the right opportunity, waiting for all the elements to fall into place before stepping out. If you are waiting for all the conditions to be ready and especially for everyone around you to like you and applaud your idea, you may never see the fulfilment of your brilliance because you will never get started. Life does not reward you because you have need and are in want but because you did something with your life. Even the good book refuses to reward laziness but delights in blessing the work of our hands. Solomon, the wisest man that ever lived, said that laziness will lead you to poverty without even trying at all. *'A little folding of the hands, a little sleep and poverty will come upon you like a thief'* and just like the accumulation of wealth, poverty is not an accident. There is a reason some people do not have money while other are super rich in the same world.

Great is the end of a matter than its beginning, therefore, become a finisher and learn to persevere against the odds. As long as we live on this planet, challenges will come, and trouble will always be a part of life for as long as the earth remains. It is not what you go through that defines you but how you deal with those challenges and how you come out of them. If you make sure that you are the last man or woman standing, it does not matter what you go through now as long as your last word is victory. It does not matter how many times you get knocked down and even consider quitting as long as you keep getting back up and live to fight another round. Time will pass whether you do something or not. I have heard people make statements like, 'I am just buying some time' or 'making up for lost time' but none of these statements carry any truth whatsoever! You can never buy more time no matter how wealthy you are, and neither can you make up for lost time. Every new minute is fresh and is an opportunity to go again, to try again and to make today count. If we could stall, then rich people would live forever because all they must do is buy the biggest chunk of time possible as live for as long as they wish. The truth is though that once time is lost, it really is gone and you will never ever get it back, so stop wasting any more of your time! Focus on the things that really matter moving forward.

What you focus on will determine what you spend your time on. Become clear about your target and goals and it will create the sense of urgency and focus that you need to use time to your advantage. If you know the result in advance, you will always ask yourself whether what you are doing right now is adding anything of value to your end-result. If it is adding no value, then you already know that you are wasting valuable time that will never ever get back no matter how sincerely sorry and well-meaning you are. It may take you some time to plan your activities to have an outcome in advance but once you have them in front of you, the results will come much quicker, and the activities in between will be easier. This can also be referred to making sure that your 'why' is bigger than anything you must do to achieve the outcome. Please remember that every day that you do not use is lost forever and can never be recovered.

FINANCIAL INDEPENDENCE

8. FINANCIAL INDEPENDENCE

Financial independence is a state of being where you have accumulated sufficient wealth and assets to sustain your desired lifestyle without the need for active employment income. It represents a level of financial security and autonomy that enables you to pursue your passions, fulfil your aspirations, and live life on your own terms. In this chapter, we explore the principles and strategies for achieving financial independence and unlocking a life of freedom and empowerment.

Financial independence is more than just having a certain amount of money in the bank; it is about having the ability to cover expenses and maintain a desired standard of living without relying on a paycheck. This state of independence provides you with the flexibility to pursue your interests, spend time with loved ones, and pursue meaningful endeavours without financial constraints, to have real freedom of choice in your finances.

Achieving financial independence begins with setting clear, measurable, and achievable financial goals. These goals may include building a retirement nest egg, paying off debt, creating multiple streams of passive income, or achieving a specific level of investment returns. By defining their objectives, you can create a roadmap for achieving financial independence and track your progress along the way, with times evaluation tools.

Embracing Frugality and Smart Spending are essential to the achievement of financial freedom. Frugality is a cornerstone of financial independence, as it involves living below or within your means, and prioritizing needs over wants. By adopting a frugal mindset and practicing smart spending habits, you can maximise your savings rate and accelerate your journey to financial independence. This may involve cutting unnecessary expenses, avoiding lifestyle inflation, and making conscious purchasing decisions aligned with your long-term financial goals.

Another key to your success is diversifying your income sources. In addition to active employment income, you can create multiple streams of passive income through investments, rental properties, royalties, dividends, and strategic side hustles. By generating income from various sources, you can reduce reliance on a sole source of income and build a resilient financial foundation that supports long-term financial independence.

Learning to invest wisely is a critical component of achieving financial independence, as it allows you to grow your wealth and generate passive income over time. Whether it involves investing in stocks, bonds, real estate, or business ventures, making informed investment decisions is essential for building wealth and achieving financial freedom. By adopting a diversified investment strategy tailored to your risk tolerance and financial goals, you can maximise returns while mitigating risk.

Once you have accumulated sufficient wealth to sustain your desired lifestyle, creating a sustainable withdrawal strategy is crucial for maintaining your financial independence. This involves determining a safe withdrawal rate from investment portfolios and retirement accounts to cover living expenses while preserving principal. By carefully managing withdrawals and adjusting spending as needed, you can ensure your financial independence lasts throughout your retirement and beyond.

Achieving financial independence is a journey that requires discipline, patience, and strategic planning. By setting clear financial goals, embracing frugality, building multiple streams of income, investing wisely, and creating a sustainable withdrawal strategy, individuals can realize their dreams of financial freedom and empowerment. Financial independence unlocks the opportunity to live life on one's own terms, pursue passions, and make a positive impact in the world. As individuals embark on this journey, they are empowered to take control of their financial futures and create a life of abundance and fulfilment.

We are living in a capitalist world and there has never been a better time in history to accumulate wealth than in our generation. If not now, then when? Believe that you can do this, you can be financially independent and find the financial freedom that you seek. Capitalism is practiced in every nation in the world today; it is a political and economic system in which trade and industry is not primarily government-run but is controlled by non-governmental business owners and investors whose main goal is to make a profit. Money Wisdom encourages you to not only complain about the capitalist world but to capitalise on it by owning a part of the world through ventures like real estate, accumulation of capital and understanding the markets and global price systems.

There are industries which would be considered saturated and even monopolised in certain countries such as the energy and transport industries. However there remains a vast array of opportunities for you to get involved in and create your own wealth in the here and now. Chances and opportunities happen to everyone at one point or the other. But like I often say, the same opportunity will embarrass you if it comes knocking when you are not ready. Focus on sharpening your gift and it will surely make room for you and make your way very prosperous as all you need for your success is already on the inside of you. We all possess the answers to our own problems and the destiny on the inside of us is what screams out in the form of desire.

It is true that some people are born into money and the world refers to them as being born with a 'silver spoon.' Regardless of how you started out though, by the time you finish reading this book, you will know how to create your own silver spoon as no one was born to be poor. Some people may have the advantage, but they also stand to lose it all if they ignore the laws that govern wealth. Instead of feeling sorry for yourself and blaming everyone around you for where you are, begin to seek out opportunities and proactively go after your dreams.

Many are the times when our failures have nothing to do with the devil or any enemies around us but have everything to do with our own failure to act correctly or even act at all. It is much better to try doing something and make mistakes along the way rather than to never try at all. One of the greatest tragedies in life is to fail because you never even tried, so whatever you must do, please do not take your brilliance to the grave. When you refuse to try, you have already lost, and you rob yourself of any chance you may have had to succeed. Therefore, fortune favours those who have the courage to try.

The world has enough resources to go around and support every single human being alive. It is, therefore, a wonder why only a handful own most of the world's resources and wealth. This uneven distribution of global wealth will never cease until the end of this world as we know it. The good news is that you will be one of the few that will cross over to the wealthy side because you have decided to do so and are already on your way to the top by seeking for answers. This world has enough resources to sustain it until its end. The problem is not a lack of resources but a lack of ideas and wisdom to convert available resources into tangible riches. Like me, have you ever wondered how some of the poorest nations in the world are also the richest in natural resources? A total stranger can go to these same nations and accumulate unimaginable wealth, proving the point that it is not a lack of resources or opportunity that keeps most people broke and in poverty but rather a lack of understanding of the wealth formula. Money is very often not the problem but a lack of ideas.

The time to sit and cry and blame everyone else is over. It is your time to move over to the rich side of life. Regardless of who is in government or where you live, you can do this. I dare you to get rich in your lifetime here on earth and not just wait for the 'sweet by and by' in paradise. Break out of containment and learn to think creatively; outside everyone's expectations. Set your own expectations and take the limits off, the only limit that really matters is the one you place on yourself. If you are waiting for everyone to like you and approve of your dreams, it might be a long time before you make any progress in your pursuit of happiness. Nobody can do what you were born to do on this planet; you are different for a reason so be happy to be a misfit, run your own race and stick to your own lane.

THE LAWS THAT GOVERN MONEY

9. THE LAWS THAT GOVERN MONEY

Money, which is a ubiquitous medium of exchange, holds immense power in shaping our lives and influencing our decisions. Yet, behind its perceived complexity lies a set of fundamental principles and laws that govern its flow, accumulation, and impact. In this chapter, we explore the laws that govern money and uncover the timeless principles that form the foundation of financial mastery.

The laws that govern money are not arbitrary; they are rooted in economic principles, behavioural psychology, and societal norms. By understanding and aligning with these laws, you can navigate the complexities of finance with clarity and purpose, paving the way for financial success and abundance.

As we look at the laws that govern money, please understand that there are more laws that control your finances. However, I have chosen to share these eighteen laws with you in the hope that they will change your life forever. Immediately after this chapter, I will proceed to break every law down further for your benefit and clarity. If you understand these laws and put them to work, you cannot remain broke and will never not have money for another day in your life as these laws will work for anyone willing to do the needful, including you:

1. **The Law of Supply and Demand**: At the core of economic theory lies the law of supply and demand, which dictates the price and availability of goods and services in a market economy. This law states that the price of a product or service is determined by the relationship between its

supply and demand. Understanding this principle is essential for your ability to make informed financial decisions, whether it involves investing in stocks, real estate, or other assets.

2. **The Law of Compounding:** The law of compounding is a powerful force in wealth creation, stating that the value of an investment grows exponentially over time as earnings generate additional earnings. This principle underscores the importance of starting early, investing consistently, and allowing investments to compound over time. By harnessing the power of compounding, you can accelerate your journey to financial freedom and build substantial wealth over the long term. The money game is all about doubling up and multiplying funds. When you make money, always ensure the money produces more of itself for you and then make the return do the same.

3. **The Law of Risk and Reward:** The law of risk and reward dictates that higher levels of risk are typically associated with higher potential returns. This principle highlights the importance of understanding and managing risk in investment decisions. While higher-risk investments may offer the potential for greater returns, they also carry a higher likelihood of loss. By diversifying investments and aligning risk with personal tolerance and financial goals, you can optimise your risk-reward ratio and achieve a balance between growth and preservation of wealth.

4. **The Law of Scarcity:** The law of scarcity emphasises the finite nature of resources and the necessity of making trade-offs in resource allocation. This principle

underscores the importance of budgeting, prioritising expenses, and living within your means. By recognising the scarcity of financial resources and making intentional choices about how to allocate them, you can optimise your financial resources and achieve greater financial stability and security.

5. **The Law of Value Creation:** The law of value creation states that wealth is created through the production of value for others. Whether through entrepreneurship, innovation, or providing valuable goods and services, creating value is essential for wealth accumulation. By focusing on creating value for others and solving pressing problems, you can generate income, build successful businesses, and create lasting wealth.

6. **Making Money vs Earning Money:** Stop working for money and make money work for you. This is the smartest way to create wealth and generate passive income for yourself over a sustained period. Money is a significant game-changer, so learn to play the game. The more you understand the money game, the more chances you must score big and win this game.

7. **The Law of Attraction:** If you respect money, it will come to you as you attract what you respect and like. This is the law of attraction. On the other hand, if you despise money, it will run away from you like a sprinter on the track.

8. **Always have a crisis account at any given time:** This is money that you do not touch no matter what because it is reserved for genuine emergencies that only you can

deal with. Resist the temptation to borrow from the crisis fund and have the discipline that it takes to win in life.

9. **Living within your means:** Do not spend what you do not have and learn to live within your means. If it is not in your budget, you cannot afford it, period. Therefore, you should always include the rainy day in your budget.

10. **Using Money as your Servant:** Cash will work for you during a crisis whether you like money or not. it is a great servant in times of trouble and a good friend to have. Just make sure that you are the boss and not the cash. Understand how other wealthy people get rich. There is somebody out there who is already doing what you want to do and enough success stories from which to learn.

11. **Give Money Direction:** Provide specific purpose and direction for your finances and stick to your own lane always, which is why it is important for you to have a financial plan. Your plan is not only your guide, but also the anchor that keeps you focused on your goal and vision; the constant that makes sure you stay in your own lane regardless of what destructions you have around you. Direction keeps you sure and steadfast.

12. **The Law of Association**: Associate with some wealthy people as you normally become like those that you hang around with. This is the law of association, and you are not immune to it like any other law.

13. **The Law of Leverage:** Leverage is key in the money game, so understand the various aspects of leveraging both with money and with people. To leverage means

being able to bend or use a situation or entity to your advantage and in this case, your advantage is profit.

14. **The Law of Seasons:** Watch the seasons of money, a big pay day for example, does not mean that you have arrived. Sometimes you will win big and sometimes you will lose, understand that the two seasons are designed to even each other out and keep you soaring high.

15. **The Law of Diversification:** Do not put all your money in one basket, study, and research more than just one opportunity or investment and learn to diversify. Money is always uncomfortable in a tight spot so let it out and give it room to spread its wings and fly high for you.

16. **Money can Make or Break you:** Money is good to you when you understand it, but it will ruin you when you abuse it due to ignorance. Do your best to get wisdom and gain understanding in your financial dealings, as without it, you will struggle to succeed. And should you manage to climb the hill of financial success and get to the top, it is wisdom and understanding that will keep you there. It takes a while to succeed sometimes but only a moment to lose it all.

17. **Money is an Amplifier:** Money does not make you happy, but it certainly helps. Money does not change you either but amplifies the character you already possess. Please do not listen to people who tell you that they do not care about money but get up every morning to go to work to earn the same money they claim not to care about.

18. **Money does not like stagnancy:** Whatever you do not use, you will lose! This principle also applies to money, if

you do not put it to work, it will disappear and may never come back to you. Money is not lazy, so put it to work.

The laws that govern money are not immutable; they are dynamic principles that reflect the interactions of individuals, markets, and economies. By understanding and aligning with these laws, you can navigate the complexities of finance with confidence and purpose, paving the way for financial success and abundance. As you apply these principles in your financial endeavours, you are empowered to create a life of prosperity, fulfilment, and impact.

THE LAW OF SUPPLY AND DEMAND

10. THE LAW OF SUPPLY AND DEMAND

The law of supply and demand is a fundamental economic principle that governs the allocation of resources and influences prices in markets. Understanding the dynamics of supply and demand is essential for your quest to create wealth and capitalise on opportunities in various sectors of the economy. In this chapter, we explore the implications of the law of supply and demand in relation to wealth creation and how you can leverage these forces to your advantage.

The law of supply and demand describes the relationship between the availability of goods or services (supply) and the desire of consumers to purchase it (demand). When demand for a product or service exceeds its supply, prices tend to rise as sellers have the upper hand. Conversely, when supply exceeds demand, prices tend to fall as sellers compete for buyers' business. Understanding the dynamics of supply and demand is crucial for identifying market opportunities and potential areas for wealth creation. By analysing trends, consumer preferences, and market conditions, you can identify underserved markets or emerging sectors with high demand and limited supply.

Whether it involves launching a new business, investing in a particular industry, or offering specialised products or services, recognising unmet demand can lead to lucrative opportunities for wealth creation. In competitive markets where supply and demand are in equilibrium, you must differentiate yourself and add value to stand out. This may involve offering unique products or services, providing exceptional customer service, or implementing innovative strategies to attract customers. By understanding consumer preferences and adapting to changing market dynamics, you can position yourself for success and thrive in competitive environments.

Supply and demand dynamics play a significant role in investment decisions across various asset classes. In the stock market, for example, investors seek to identify companies with strong demand for their products or services and limited supply of shares. Similarly, in real estate investing, individuals look for properties in areas with high demand and limited supply, driving property values and rental income. By understanding and aligning investment decisions with supply and demand fundamentals, you can generate attractive returns and capitalise on the inefficiencies in the market.

The law of supply and demand underscores the importance of creating value for others in wealth creation. By addressing unmet needs, solving problems, and delivering products or services that resonate with consumers, you can generate demand and command premium prices. Whether through entrepreneurship, or innovation, creating value is a cornerstone of wealth creation that drives demand and fosters long-term success.

The law of supply and demand is a powerful force in wealth creation that shapes market dynamics and influences economic outcomes. By understanding these principles and leveraging supply and demand dynamics to your advantage, you can identify opportunities, make informed investment decisions, and create value in various sectors of the economy. Whether as an entrepreneur, investor, or professional, aligning with the forces of supply and demand empowers you to achieve your financial goals and build lasting wealth.

THE LAW OF COMPOUNDING

11. THE LAW OF COMPOUNDING

The law of compounding is a fundamental principle in wealth creation that highlights the power of time and consistent growth to multiply financial assets exponentially. Understanding and harnessing the concept of compounding is essential for your search for long-term wealth and achievement of financial freedom. In this chapter, we explore the profound impact of the law of compounding in wealth creation and how you can leverage this principle to your advantage. Money is a doubling game and what you do with it matters more than its acquisition.

The law of compounding, often attributed to Albert Einstein as the "eighth wonder of the world," refers to the process by which an asset's earnings generate additional earnings over time, leading to exponential growth. Compound interest is the most common application of this principle, where the interest earned on an initial investment is reinvested, leading to accelerated growth of the investment over time.

Harnessing the power of compound interest is a game-changer. Compound interest is a powerful force in wealth creation that allows investments to grow exponentially over time. By reinvesting earnings and allowing investments to compound, you can accelerate your journey to financial independence and build substantial wealth. The key to maximising the power of compound interest is to start early, invest consistently, and maintain a long-term perspective to allow compounding to work.

The time horizon plays a crucial role in the effectiveness of compound interest in wealth creation. The longer the investment horizon, the greater the impact of compounding on wealth accumulation. By starting early and allowing investments to compound over several decades, individuals can harness the full potential of compounding and achieve significant financial growth, even with modest initial investments.

Consistency is essential in harnessing the power of compound interest. Regular contributions to investment accounts, such as retirement accounts or brokerage accounts, allow you to benefit from continuous compounding over time. By making consistent contributions and reinvesting dividends or interest earnings, you can accelerate wealth accumulation and achieve your financial goals and objectives sooner.

Diversification is important in wealth creation to mitigate risk and enhance the effectiveness of compounding. By spreading investments across a diversified portfolio of assets, you can reduce the impact of market volatility and achieve more stable, consistent returns over time. Additionally, prudent risk management strategies, such as periodic rebalancing and asset allocation adjustments, help to optimise investment performance and maximise the benefits of compounding.

Start Now, because the most important aspect of harnessing the power of compounding is to start now. Regardless of your age or financial situation, the sooner you begin investing and allowing your assets to compound, the greater the potential for wealth accumulation. By acting today and making consistent, disciplined contributions to investment accounts, you can set yourself on a path towards financial independence and long-term wealth.

The law of compounding is a powerful force in wealth creation that underscores the importance of time, consistency, and discipline in achieving financial success. By understanding and harnessing the concept of compounding, you can accelerate your journey to financial independence, build substantial wealth over time, and achieve your long-term financial goals. Whether through regular contributions to investment accounts, prudent risk management, or a long-term investment perspective, leveraging the power of compounding empowers you to create a future of financial abundance and security.

THE LAW OF RISK AND REWARD

12. THE LAW OF RISK AND REWARD

The law of risk and reward is a fundamental principle in wealth creation that highlights the relationship between the level of risk taken and the potential for reward. Understanding this principle is essential for individuals seeking to build wealth and achieve their financial goals. In this chapter, we explore the dynamics of the law of risk and reward in wealth creation and how you can navigate this balance to optimise your financial outcomes.

The law of risk and reward states that higher levels of risk are typically associated with higher potential rewards, while lower levels of risk are associated with lower potential rewards. This principle reflects the trade-off individuals must consider when making financial decisions, weighing the potential for gain against the possibility of loss.

One of the first steps in navigating the law of risk and reward is to assess your own risk tolerance. Risk tolerance refers to your ability and willingness to withstand fluctuations in the value of your investments and tolerate potential losses. Understanding your risk tolerance is crucial for aligning investment decisions with your personal comfort levels and financial goals.

Diversification is a key strategy for managing risk in wealth creation. By spreading investments across a diverse portfolio of assets, you can reduce the impact of volatility in any single investment and minimise the risk of significant losses. Diversification allows you to capture the potential for growth in different sectors of the economy while mitigating the risk of concentrated exposure to any particular asset class.

The law of risk and reward requires that you strike a balance between your appetite for risk and your desired level of return. Higher-risk investments, such as stocks or venture capital, offer the potential for greater returns but also carry a higher likelihood of volatility and loss. Lower-risk investments, such as bonds or savings accounts, offer more stability but typically yield lower returns. By aligning investment decisions with personal risk tolerance and financial goals, you can optimise the risk-return profile of your investment portfolio.

The time horizon is another key factor to consider when managing risk in wealth creation. Individuals with longer time horizons may be able to tolerate higher levels of risk in their investment portfolios, as they have more time to weather market fluctuations and recover from potential losses. Conversely, individuals with shorter time horizons may opt for more conservative investment strategies to preserve capital and protect against short-term market volatility. Your goal is to make sure that you are on the right side of this equation.

Navigating the law of risk and reward requires continual assessment and adjustment of investment strategies. Market conditions, economic factors, and personal circumstances may change over time, necessitating adjustments to investment portfolios and risk management strategies. Regularly reviewing and rebalancing investment portfolios allows you to adapt to changing market dynamics and optimise your risk-return profile.

The law of risk and reward is an essential principle in wealth creation that highlights the importance of balancing risk and return in investment decisions. By understanding one's risk tolerance, diversifying investment portfolios, and aligning investment decisions with personal financial goals, you can navigate the complexities of risk and reward to optimise your financial outcomes. Navigating the law of risk and reward requires discipline, diligence, and a willingness to adapt to changing market conditions, but by doing so, you can achieve your long-term financial goals and build lasting wealth.

THE LAW OF SCARCITY

13. THE LAW OF SCARCITY

The law of scarcity is an essential principle in economics that states that limited resources must be allocated among competing uses. In the context of wealth creation and money wisdom, understanding and embracing the concept of scarcity can lead to a mindset shift towards abundance, fostering wise financial decisions and wealth accumulation. In this chapter, we explore the implications of the law of scarcity in relation to wealth creation and money wisdom, and how you can leverage this principle to achieve your financial success.

The law of scarcity underscores the finite nature of resources, including time, money, and opportunities, in the face of unlimited wants and needs. This principle highlights the need for you to make choices and trade-offs in allocating your resources effectively to maximise your utility and achieve your goals. While the law of scarcity emphasises the limitations of resources, embracing an abundance mindset is essential for wealth creation and money wisdom. An abundance mindset is characterised by a belief in the abundance of opportunities, possibilities, and resources available to you. By shifting your mindset from scarcity to abundance, you can overcome limiting beliefs and open yourself up to new possibilities for financial growth and success.

The law of scarcity requires that you prioritise your resources based on your values, goals, and priorities. This may involve making trade-offs between competing uses of time, money, and energy to allocate resources in a manner that aligns with your long-term objectives. By prioritising resources effectively, you can optimise your efforts towards wealth creation and achieve greater financial success. In the face of limited resources, practicing financial discipline is essential for wealth creation and money wisdom. Financial discipline involves living within or below your means, avoiding unnecessary expenses, and prioritising savings and investments for long-term financial goals.

By exercising discipline in managing resources, you can build a solid financial foundation and position yourself for future wealth accumulation. While scarcity may present challenges however, it also creates opportunities for wealth creation and innovation. Recognizing and leveraging scarcity-driven opportunities can lead to innovative solutions, new business ventures, and value creation. By identifying unmet needs and addressing scarcity in the market, you can capitalise on opportunities for financial success. During scarcity, cultivating gratitude and contentment is essential for money wisdom and overall well-being. Gratitude involves appreciating the resources and opportunities available, regardless of your perceived scarcity.

By cultivating gratitude and contentment, you can shift your focus from what you lack to what they have, leading to greater success in your financial journey. The law of scarcity serves as a reminder of the finite nature of resources and the need for you to make choices and trade-offs in allocating your resources effectively. By embracing an abundance mindset, prioritising resources, practicing financial discipline, leveraging scarcity for opportunity, and cultivating gratitude and contentment, you can navigate the complexities of wealth creation and money wisdom with clarity and purpose. By leveraging the principles of scarcity and abundance, you can and will achieve financial success.

THE LAW OF VALUE CREATION

14. THE LAW OF VALUE CREATION

The law of value creation is a foundational principle in business and wealth creation, emphasising the importance of delivering meaningful value to customers and stakeholders. In today's competitive landscape, businesses that prioritise value creation are not only more likely to succeed but also have the potential to generate substantial wealth. In this chapter, we explore the significance of the law of value creation in relation to the creation of wealth and business success. The law of value creation asserts that sustainable wealth is built through the creation of value for others. Whether through products, services, or solutions, businesses that prioritize delivering tangible benefits to their customers and stakeholders have a greater likelihood of long-term success and profitability.

The first step in value creation is identifying unmet needs or pain points in the market. Successful businesses are founded on the premise of addressing specific challenges or providing solutions that improve the lives of your target customers. By conducting market research, gathering feedback, and understanding customer preferences, you can identify opportunities for value creation and develop products or services that meet genuine market needs. Value creation often hinges on differentiation and innovation. Successful businesses distinguish themselves from competitors by offering unique value propositions, innovative features, or superior quality.

By continuously innovating and refining your offerings based on customer feedback and market trends, you can stay ahead of the curve and maintain a competitive edge in the market. A customer-centric approach is essential for value creation and business success. By prioritising the needs, preferences, and satisfaction of their customers, businesses can build strong relationships, foster brand loyalty, and drive repeat business. Listening to customer feedback, addressing concerns, and consistently delivering value-added experiences are key strategies for creating lasting value and building a loyal customer base. Customer retention is critical to sustainable success.

Value creation is not just about meeting immediate needs; it is about creating sustainable solutions that provide long-term benefits to customers and stakeholders. Businesses that prioritise sustainability, ethical practices, and social responsibility are increasingly valued by consumers and investors alike. By incorporating environmental, social, and governance (ESG) considerations into your operations, you can create value while making a positive impact on society and the planet.

As businesses grow and expand, they can scale their impact and create value on a larger scale. Whether through geographic expansion, diversification of product offerings, or strategic partnerships, scaling allows businesses to reach new markets, serve more customers, and drive revenue growth. By leveraging technology, automation, and scalable business models, you can amplify your impact and create wealth through value creation.

The law of value creation is a guiding principle for entrepreneurs and businesses seeking to build wealth and achieve success. By prioritising the delivery of meaningful value to customers and stakeholders, businesses can differentiate themselves, foster loyalty, and drive sustainable growth. Whether through innovation, customer-centricity, sustainability, or scalability, value creation lies at the heart of successful business ventures and wealth creation. As you embrace the law of value creation, you are empowered to create lasting impact, drive financial prosperity, and build a business that will thrive in all seasons.

MAKING MONEY

VS

EARNING MONEY

15. MAKING MONEY VS EARNING MONEY

There is a huge difference between making money and earning money. In the pursuit of financial success, you will often encounter the distinction between making money and earning money. While these terms are sometimes used interchangeably, they represent distinct approaches to wealth accumulation and financial empowerment. In this chapter, we explore the differences between making money and earning money, and how understanding this distinction can lead to more informed financial decisions and greater long-term prosperity.

Making money and earning money are two distinct approaches to generating income, each with its own implications for wealth creation and financial independence. Making money typically refers to generating income through entrepreneurial endeavours, investments, or other non-traditional means. This may involve starting a business, investing in real estate or stocks, creating intellectual property, or pursuing other innovative ventures. Making money often requires creativity, risk-taking, and a willingness to be creative to identify lucrative opportunities for wealth creation. While making money can lead to significant financial rewards, it also entails a higher degree of uncertainty and risk compared to traditional forms of employment.

Earning money, on the other hand, typically refers to generating income through traditional employment or conventional means. This may involve working for an employer, receiving a salary or hourly wage, or earning commissions or bonuses through employment-related activities. Earning money provides a more predictable and stable source of income compared to making money, as it is often tied to regular employment or contractual arrangements. While earning money may offer less potential for rapid wealth accumulation compared to making money, it provides a reliable source of income and financial security for many individuals. I often say, get a job if you must, while you pursue your business ideas until they can pay your bills.

Understanding the Pros and Cons of the two is critical to your financial success. Both making money and earning money have their own set of advantages and disadvantages, and the choice between the two depends on individual preferences, goals, and risk tolerance. Here are the key differences I have identified:

Pros of Making Money:

- Greater potential for high returns and rapid wealth accumulation.

- Opportunities for entrepreneurial creativity and innovation.

- Flexibility and autonomy in managing one's income-generating activities.

- Ability to leverage assets, investments, and business ventures for financial growth.

Cons of Making Money:

- Higher degree of risk and uncertainty compared to traditional employment.

- Requires significant upfront investment of time, resources, and capital.

- Potential for failure or loss in entrepreneurial ventures or investments.
- Limited access to benefits and stability typically associated with traditional employment.

Pros of Earning Money:

- Predictable and stable source of income with regular pay checks or compensation.
- Access to benefits such as health insurance, retirement plans, and paid time off.
- Opportunities for career advancement, skill development, and professional growth.
- Lower risk compared to entrepreneurial ventures or investment activities.

Cons of Earning Money:

- Limited potential for rapid wealth accumulation compared to entrepreneurial endeavours or investments.
- Reliance on employers and external factors for income generation.
- Potential for income stagnation or limited earning potential in certain professions or industries.
- Less flexibility and autonomy compared to self-employment or entrepreneurial activities.

Understanding the distinction between making money and earning money is essential for your achievement financial success and long-term prosperity. While both approaches have their own set of advantages and disadvantages, the choice between making money and earning money depends on individual preferences, goals, and risk tolerance. By carefully weighing the pros and cons of each approach, you can make informed financial decisions that align with your unique circumstances and aspirations. Whether through entrepreneurial endeavours, investments or traditional employment, the key to financial success lies in leveraging opportunities, managing risks, and pursuing a path that leads to greater empowerment and financial freedom.

THE LAW OF ATTRACTION

16. THE LAW OF ATTRACTION

The law of attraction is a powerful principle that suggests individuals can attract into their lives whatever they focus on and believe in. While often associated with personal development and spiritual growth, the law of attraction also has profound implications for creating wealth and cultivating money wisdom. In this chapter, we explore the relationship between the law of attraction and financial success, and how you can harness this principle to manifest wealth and cultivate money wisdom.

The law of attraction is based on the premise that like attracts like, and that individuals have the power to manifest their desires through focused intention, belief, and visualisation. According to this principle, thoughts and beliefs can shape reality, and you can attract positive outcomes into your life by aligning your thoughts and emotions with your desired goals and outcomes. In the context of wealth creation, this involves cultivating a mindset of abundance, prosperity, and financial empowerment.

By focusing on positive thoughts and beliefs about money, you can shift your mindset from scarcity and limitation to abundance and possibility, opening yourself up to opportunities for wealth creation and financial success. Visualisation is a powerful technique used in the practice of the law of attraction to manifest desired outcomes. By visualising yourself achieving your financial goals, you can create a mental blueprint of success and reinforce your belief in your ability to create wealth. Visualisation helps you align your thoughts, emotions, and actions with your desired outcomes, making it more likely for you to attract opportunities and resources that support our financial goals and objectives.

Practicing gratitude is an essential component of the law of attraction and plays a crucial role in manifesting wealth and financial abundance. By cultivating a sense of gratitude for the resources, opportunities, and abundance already present in your life, you can attract even more blessings and prosperity into your experience. Practicing gratitude helps you shift your focus from what you lack to what you have, creating a positive energy that attracts more abundance and opportunities for wealth creation.

While the law of attraction emphasises the power of thoughts and beliefs in manifesting desired outcomes, it also emphasises the importance of taking inspired action towards your goals. This involves aligning your actions with your intentions and beliefs and taking proactive steps towards achieving your financial objectives. By combining positive thoughts and beliefs with inspired action, you can manifest your desires and create tangible results in your financial journey. Talk alone is cheap, and your action is key.

The law of attraction also extends to cultivating money wisdom, which involves making wise financial decisions and managing resources responsibly. By aligning thoughts and beliefs with principles of financial wisdom, such as budgeting, saving, investing, and avoiding debt, you can attract financial abundance and create a solid foundation for long-term wealth creation. Money wisdom involves being mindful of your financial decisions and cultivating a positive relationship with money based on empowerment, abundance, and prosperity.

The law of attraction is a powerful principle that has the potential to transform your life forever and create wealth and abundance in all areas of your life, including your finances. By aligning thoughts and beliefs with desired outcomes, visualising success, practicing gratitude, taking inspired action, and cultivating money wisdom, you can harness the power of the law of attraction to manifest your financial goals and create a life of abundance, prosperity, and financial empowerment. As you embrace the principles of the law of attraction in your financial journey, you are empowered to attract wealth, cultivate money wisdom, and create a legacy of prosperity for yourself and future generations.

THE EMERGENCY (CRISIS) FUND

17. THE EMERGENCY (CRISIS) FUND

The emergency or crisis fund is designed for the "rainy day" that comes to all of us some day in our lives. In the pursuit of wealth creation, individuals often focus on strategies for increasing income, building investments, and growing assets. However, one crucial aspect that is often overlooked is the importance of having an emergency or crisis fund. An emergency fund serves as a financial safety net, providing you with a buffer against unexpected expenses, financial emergencies, and unforeseen crises. In this chapter, we explore the significance of having an emergency or crisis fund in relation to wealth creation and financial security.

An emergency or crisis fund acts as a safety net to protect you against financial setbacks that may occur unexpectedly. Whether it is a medical emergency, job loss, car repair, or home maintenance issue, having a dedicated fund set aside for emergencies allows you to cover these expenses without resorting to high-interest debt or depleting long-term savings and investments. Having an emergency fund helps you avoid relying on credit cards, loans, or other forms of debt to cover unexpected expenses. By having cash reserves readily available, you can avoid accruing high-interest charges and debt repayment obligations, which can erode wealth over time and hinder financial progress.

Knowing that there is a financial safety net in place provides you with peace of mind and reduces stress during times of uncertainty or crisis. Instead of worrying about how to cover unexpected expenses, you can focus on addressing the situation effectively and proactively, leading to better decision-making and overall wellbeing. And this also includes your mental health wellbeing. An emergency or crisis fund helps preserve long-term investments and assets by providing a source of liquidity during times of need. Without an emergency fund, you may be forced to sell investments prematurely or incur penalties for early withdrawals from retirement accounts, which can hinder wealth accumulation and jeopardise your financial goals.

Having an emergency or crisis fund in place allows you to take advantage of opportunities for growth and wealth creation without risking your financial security. Whether it is investing in a promising business venture, seizing a lucrative investment opportunity, or pursuing further education or professional development, having cash reserves provides you with the flexibility to capitalise on opportunities for financial advancement. An emergency or crisis fund is a critical component of wealth creation and financial security. By setting aside funds for unexpected expenses, you can protect yourself against financial setbacks, avoid debt and interest charges, reduce stress, preserve long-term investments, and seize opportunities for growth and wealth creation. While the amount of an emergency fund may vary depending on your circumstances, having one in place is essential for achieving long-term financial stability and success. As you prioritize building and maintaining an emergency or crisis fund, you can enhance your financial resilience, protect your wealth, and achieve your goals with greater confidence and peace of mind that you cannot place a price on.

LIVING WITHIN YOUR MEANS

18. LIVING WITHIN YOUR MEANS

Living within or below your means is a foundational law of personal finance that forms the cornerstone of wealth creation. By practicing frugality, budgeting effectively, and prioritising financial discipline, you can maximise your savings, reduce debt, and build wealth over time. In this chapter, we explore the importance of living within your means in creating wealth and achieving long-term financial success.

Living within your means involves aligning your expenses with your income and avoiding overspending or living beyond your financial capabilities. This requires a conscious effort to prioritise needs over wants, make intentional financial decisions, and live a lifestyle that is sustainable and affordable based on your income level. Living within your means allows you to maximise your savings and investments by allocating a portion of your income towards wealth-building activities.

By consistently saving a percentage of your income, you can accumulate funds for emergencies, investments, retirement, and other long-term financial goals. Additionally, living within your means enables you to avoid unnecessary expenses and redirect those funds towards investments that generate passive income and accelerate wealth creation.

Living within your means helps you avoid accumulating excessive debt and financial obligations that can hinder wealth creation and cause financial stress. By prioritising debt repayment and avoiding high-interest debt, you can free up more disposable income for savings and investments, thereby accelerating wealth accumulation. Additionally, living within or below your means reduces financial stress by ensuring that you have a financial cushion to cover unexpected expenses and emergencies without resorting to borrowing or tapping into savings. It requires cultivating financial discipline and adopting responsible financial habits. This involves creating and sticking to a budget, tracking expenses, avoiding impulse purchases, and making informed financial decisions based on long-term goals rather than short-term gratification.

By practicing financial discipline, you can control your spending, prioritise savings, and stay on track towards achieving your financial objectives. Embracing a minimalist lifestyle is a powerful way to live within your means and accelerate wealth creation. Minimalism involves decluttering your life, focusing on essential possessions, and prioritising experiences and relationships over material possessions. By simplifying your lifestyle, you can reduce expenses, free up resources for savings and investments, and cultivate a greater sense of fulfilment and contentment that transcends material wealth.

Living within your means is a fundamental principle of wealth creation that empowers you to take control of your finances, maximise savings and investments, reduce debt, and cultivate financial discipline. By aligning expenses with income, prioritising needs over wants, and adopting a minimalist mindset, you can accelerate wealth creation, achieve long-term financial security, and create a life of abundance and fulfilment. As you embrace the principles of living within your means, you can build a solid financial foundation, pursue your goals with confidence, and realise your vision of financial independence and prosperity.

USING MONEY AS YOUR SERVANT

19. USING MONEY AS YOUR SERVANT

Money, when managed effectively, can serve as a powerful tool for wealth creation and financial empowerment. By understanding the principles of money management, you can leverage financial resources to generate income, build assets, and achieve your long-term financial goals. In this chapter, we explore the concept of using money as your servant in the creation of wealth and how you can harness the power of financial resources to build lasting prosperity. Money Wisdom is designed to help you understand how to make money work for you, instead of you working for money. It is designed to help you stop trading your time for money and instead start trading money for money.

Money is a tool to be used as your servant. It is essential to shift your mindset and view money as a tool rather than a master. Instead of being controlled by money or allowing it to dictate your life, view money as a resource that you can leverage to achieve your goals and aspirations. By adopting a mindset of abundance and empowerment, you can harness the power of financial resources to create wealth and build a life of plenty.

Investing for passive income is one of the most effective ways to use money as your servant. Passive income streams, such as rental properties, dividend-paying stocks, or royalties from intellectual property, allow you to generate income without actively trading your time for money. By investing your money wisely in income-producing assets, you can build a source of passive income that continues to grow and support your financial goals over time. This is money you make while you are sleeping.

Creating multiple streams of income using money as your servant involves diversifying your income streams and creating multiple sources of revenue. By building diverse income streams, such as side businesses, freelance work, rental properties, or online ventures, you can reduce reliance on any sole source of income and increase your overall financial resilience. Multiple streams of income provide stability and security while also unlocking greater potential for wealth creation and financial freedom.

Automating Financial Systems To effectively use money as your servant, it is crucial to automate your financial systems and processes. Set up automatic contributions to savings and investment accounts, automate bill payments, and use technology to track expenses and monitor financial progress. By automating your finances, you can streamline money management tasks, minimise manual intervention, and ensure that your financial resources are working efficiently to support your wealth creation goals.

Using money as your servant is a mindset shift that empowers individuals to take control of their financial destinies and build lasting wealth. By viewing money as a tool for achieving goals, investing for passive income, leveraging debt strategically, creating multiple streams of income, and automating financial systems, you can harness the power of financial resources to create a life of abundance, prosperity, and plenty. As you embrace the principles of using money as your servant, you can unlock your full financial potential, achieve your dreams, and build a legacy of prosperity for generations to come.

THE LAW OF DIRECTION

20. THE LAW OF DIRECTION

The law of direction emphasizes the importance of clarity, focus, and purpose in achieving financial success. By setting clear goals, developing a strategic plan, and taking intentional actions, you can harness the power of direction to create wealth and cultivate money wisdom. In this chapter, we explore how the law of direction influences wealth creation and the role it plays in guiding individuals towards financial abundance and prosperity.

The first step in harnessing the power of direction is to set clear financial goals. These goals serve as a roadmap for wealth creation, providing a sense of direction and purpose in your financial journey. Whether it is achieving a specific net worth, saving for retirement, purchasing a home, or starting a business, clear financial goals provide clarity and focus, guiding you towards your desired outcomes.

Once clear goals are established, the next step is to develop a strategic financial plan to achieve them. A financial plan outlines specific steps, timelines, and milestones for achieving financial goals, considering factors such as income, expenses, investments, and risk tolerance. By developing a strategic plan, you can align your actions with your goals, prioritise resources effectively, and stay on track towards financial success.

The law of direction emphasises the importance of taking intentional actions aligned with your financial goals. This involves making conscious decisions about spending, saving, investing, and managing resources in a way that supports long-term financial objectives. By taking intentional actions, you can make progress towards your goals, overcome obstacles, and stay focused on your path to wealth creation.

Direction in wealth creation also involves cultivating financial discipline and staying committed to the plan, even in the face of challenges or temptations. This requires practicing habits such as budgeting, saving, investing consistently, and avoiding unnecessary expenses. By cultivating financial discipline, individuals can stay focused on their goals, resist impulsive decisions, and stay on course towards achieving financial success.

While having a clear direction is important, it is also essential to be flexible and adaptable in response to changing circumstances or new opportunities. This may involve reassessing goals, adjusting the financial plan, or pivoting strategies based on evolving priorities or market conditions. By remaining open to new possibilities and willing to adjust course as needed, you can navigate challenges, seize opportunities, and continue moving forward on your path to wealth creation.

The law of direction is a powerful principle that guides you towards financial success by providing clarity, focus, and purpose in your wealth creation journey. By setting clear goals, developing a strategic plan, taking intentional actions, cultivating financial discipline, and adjusting course as needed, you can harness the power of direction to create wealth, achieve financial independence, and cultivate money wisdom. As you align your actions with your goals and stay focused on your path, the path I often call "Own Lane", you can unlock your full financial potential and create a life of abundance and prosperity.

THE LAW OF ASSOCIATION

21. THE LAW OF ASSOCIATION

The law of association emphasises the profound impact that relationships and connections have on your success and achievement of financial freedom. By surrounding yourself with like-minded individuals, mentors, and strategic partners, you can leverage the power of association to accelerate wealth creation, expand opportunities, and cultivate financial wisdom. In this chapter, we explore the role of the law of association in relation to financial freedom and wealth creation, and how you can harness the power of your social networks to achieve your financial goals and objectives.

The law of association suggests that individuals tend to adopt the attitudes, behaviours, and habits of the people they spend the most time with. By surrounding yourself with successful, ambitious individuals who prioritise financial freedom and wealth creation, you can elevate your own mindset, motivation, and aspirations. Being part of a supportive and inspiring social circle can provide encouragement, accountability, and valuable insights that propel you towards your financial goals.

Association with mentors is key to your success. Mentorship is a powerful tool for wealth creation and personal growth. By seeking guidance and wisdom from mentors who have achieved financial success, you can benefit from their knowledge, experience, and perspective. Mentors can provide valuable advice, share strategies for wealth creation, and offer support and encouragement along the journey. Learning from the experiences of mentors and role models can inspire you to overcome challenges, take calculated risks, and pursue opportunities for financial growth.

Strategic relationships are essential for wealth creation and financial freedom. By building relationships with individuals who possess complementary skills, resources, or expertise, you can unlock new opportunities for collaboration, joint ventures, and mutual support. Strategic partners can provide access to networks, capital, and opportunities that you may not have on your own, accelerating your path towards financial success.

Networking and community engagement are valuable tools for expanding your social capital and accessing opportunities for wealth creation. By actively participating in networking events, industry conferences, and community organisations, you can build relationships with like-minded professionals, entrepreneurs, and investors. Networking provides opportunities to exchange ideas, share knowledge, and forge valuable connections that can lead to partnerships, collaborations, and business opportunities conducive to wealth creation.

The law of association underscores the importance of cultivating a positive and supportive environment that fosters growth, collaboration, and mutual empowerment. By surrounding yourself with individuals who share similar values, goals, and aspirations, you can create a culture of positivity, encouragement, and mutual support that fuels your journey towards financial freedom and wealth creation.

The law of association is a powerful principle that underscores the impact of relationships and social networks on your success. By surrounding yourself with success-oriented individuals, learning from mentors and role models, building strategic relationships, engaging in networking activities, and cultivating a positive and supportive environment, you can leverage the power of association to accelerate your path towards financial success. As you harness the power of your social networks and build meaningful relationships, you can unlock new opportunities, overcome obstacles, and achieve your goals with greater clarity, confidence, and resilience. It is famously said that if you want to know the type of person you are, just check out the company that you keep, because you become like the people you hang out with.

THE LAW OF LEVERAGE

22. THE LAW OF LEVERAGE

The law of leverage is a powerful principle in wealth creation that emphasises the strategic use of resources to amplify financial outcomes. By harnessing the power of leverage, you can multiply your efforts, resources, and opportunities to accelerate wealth creation and cultivate financial wisdom. In this chapter, we explore the concept of the law of leverage and how you can use it to create wealth in alignment with financial wisdom. The law of leverage involves maximising the impact of resources through strategic utilisation and optimisation. Leverage allows you to achieve greater results with less effort or resources by effectively leveraging assets, relationships, skills, and opportunities. In the context of wealth creation, leverage enables you to multiply your financial gains, accelerate growth, and achieve financial freedom more efficiently.

One of the most common forms of leverage in wealth creation is financial leverage, which involves using borrowed funds or financial instruments to amplify returns on investment. Examples of financial leverage include using leverage in real estate investments through mortgages, leveraging margin accounts in stock trading, or using loans to finance business ventures. While financial leverage can amplify gains, it is essential to use it judiciously and manage risks effectively to avoid excessive debt and financial instability.

Another form of leverage in wealth creation involves leveraging skills, expertise, and knowledge to create value and generate income. you can leverage your unique talents, strengths, and expertise to build successful businesses, freelance careers, or consulting practices. By honing your skills and leveraging your expertise, you can create high-value products, services, or solutions that command premium prices and generate sustainable income streams.

Relationships and networks are powerful forms of leverage that can unlock new opportunities, access resources, and accelerate wealth creation. By building strong relationships with mentors, advisors, strategic partners, and influencers, you can leverage your networks to gain valuable insights, access capital, and expand your reach in the marketplace. Networking and relationship-building provide opportunities for collaboration, joint ventures, and referrals that can amplify financial outcomes and propel you towards your financial goals.

Time is a valuable resource that can be leveraged to create wealth effectively. By optimising time management, prioritising high-impact activities, and automating repetitive tasks, you can free up more time to focus on income-generating activities, personal development, and strategic planning. Automation tools, technology, and systems can streamline processes, increase efficiency, and amplify productivity, enabling you to achieve more in less time and accelerate wealth creation.

The law of leverage is a powerful principle that empowers you to amplify your efforts, resources, and opportunities in wealth creation. By strategically leveraging financial resources, skills and expertise, relationships and networks, and time and automation, you can multiply your financial gains, accelerate growth, and achieve financial freedom with greater efficiency and effectiveness. As you harness the power of leverage and apply it in alignment with financial wisdom, they can create wealth, build a legacy of prosperity, and live a life of abundance and plenty. A wise proverb says that "no man is an island," and there is a Zambian proverb that says, "It takes a whole village to raise a child." The impact is the same in both cases, we were never designed to do life on our own and the power of leverage cannot be overemphasised. And while I am quoting proverbs, here is one more African proverb known as Ubuntu, which says, "I am because we are." This proverb about Ubuntu is a philosophy originating from the Nguni Bantu languages of Southern Africa, particularly Zulu and Xhosa. It is often translated as "I am because we are" or "humanity towards others." This proverb encapsulates the interconnectedness of humanity and the belief that individuals are defined by their relationships with others in the community. It emphasises the importance of empathy, compassion, and mutual respect in human interactions, highlighting the idea that one's humanity is affirmed through their relationships and actions towards others. Ubuntu underscores the notion that individuals thrive when they recognise and uphold the inherent dignity and worth of every person, contributing to the well-being and prosperity of the community. Ubuntu fully encapsulates the law of leverage.

THE LAW OF SEASONS

23. THE LAW OF SEASONS

The law of seasons teaches us that life and wealth creation unfold in cycles, characterised by periods of growth, harvest, dormancy, and renewal. By understanding and embracing the rhythms of these seasons, you can cultivate patience, adaptability, and resilience in your financial journey. One of my favourite sayings is that life is not a straight line, that it is not linear in any way. In this chapter, we explore the law of seasons in relation to the creation of wealth and money wisdom, and how you can navigate these cycles to achieve long-term financial success regardless of the ever-changing seasons of life.

Just as nature experiences seasons of growth, you will experience periods of growth in your wealth creation journey. During these seasons, opportunities abound, and you can focus on expanding your income, investments, and assets. It is essential to seize these opportunities and capitalise on favourable market conditions, economic trends, and personal strengths to maximise growth and accelerate wealth creation.

After periods of growth come seasons of harvest, where you get to reap the rewards of your efforts and investments. During these seasons, you get to enjoy the fruits of your labour, whether through increased income, investment returns, or business profits. It is crucial to celebrate successes, acknowledge achievements, and make strategic decisions about reinvesting profits, diversifying assets, and preserving wealth for the future.

And just as nature experiences seasons of dormancy, you may encounter periods of stagnation or consolidation in your wealth creation journey. During these seasons, economic downturns, market corrections, or personal challenges may temporarily slow progress and require patience and perseverance. It is essential to remain steadfast, focus on preserving capital, and use this time for reflection, learning, and strategic planning to prepare for the next season of growth. Some of the greatest lessons I have ever learnt in life came during the most difficult of times. And sometimes, we only realise the true meaning of life's experiences long after the incident has passed. We indeed live and learn.

After periods of dormancy come seasons of renewal, where you emerge stronger, wiser, and more resilient. These seasons provide opportunities for reflection, innovation, and reinvention, as you adapt to changing circumstances, seize new opportunities, and embark on fresh beginnings. It is crucial to embrace change, stay agile, and leverage lessons learned to position yourself for growth and success in the next season of wealth creation.

The law of seasons teaches us the importance of patience and adaptability in wealth creation. Patience allows you to navigate the inevitable difficulties of the financial markets, resist impulsive decisions, and stay focused on long-term goals. Adaptability enables you to adjust strategies, pivot when necessary, and seize opportunities in changing market conditions. By embracing patience and adaptability, you can navigate the law of seasons with confidence and resilience, achieving sustainable wealth creation and cultivating money wisdom.

The law of seasons reminds us that wealth creation is a journey characterised by cycles of growth, harvest, dormancy, and renewal. By understanding and embracing these seasons, you can cultivate patience, adaptability, and resilience in your financial journey, navigating challenges and seizing opportunities with wisdom and foresight. As you align your actions with the rhythms of the law of seasons, you can achieve long-term financial success, build lasting wealth, and create a legacy of prosperity for generations to come.

Triumph over the difficulties of life is a testament to the resilience, strength, and determination that lies within everyone. It signifies the ability to navigate through challenges, setbacks, and uncertainties with courage, perseverance, and optimism. Triumph is not merely about overcoming obstacles, but also about learning and growing from experiences, finding inner strength during times of adversity, and emerging stronger, wiser, and more resilient. It reflects the human spirit's capacity to rise above hardships, embrace change, and forge a path towards greater fulfilment, success, and true happiness.

THE LAW OF DIVERSIFICATION

24. THE LAW OF DIVERSIFICATION

The law of diversification is a Key principle in wealth creation that emphasises the importance of spreading risk and maximising opportunities through strategic allocation of resources. By diversifying investments, income streams, and assets, individuals can minimize exposure to volatility and uncertainty while maximising long-term returns. In this chapter, we explore the law of diversification in relation to the creation of wealth and money wisdom, and how you can leverage diversification to achieve financial success.

The law of diversification suggests that spreading investments across a variety of assets, industries, and markets can reduce risk and enhance returns over time. Diversification helps mitigate the impact of volatility, market fluctuations, and unforeseen events by ensuring that losses in one area are offset by gains in others. By diversifying investments, you can achieve a balance between risk and reward, optimising your portfolio for long-term growth and stability along the way.

One of the key applications of the law of diversification is in investment portfolios. Rather than putting all eggs in one basket, you can spread your investments across different asset classes, such as stocks, bonds, real estate, and alternative investments. Within each asset class, further diversification can be achieved by investing in a variety of securities, sectors, and geographic regions. Diversifying investment portfolios helps reduce exposure to market risk and volatility, providing a more stable foundation for wealth creation over time.

In addition to diversifying investment portfolios, you can also diversify your income streams to enhance financial security and resilience. Relying solely on an only source of income, such as a job or business, exposes you to the risk of income loss in the event of job loss, economic downturns, or industry disruptions. By diversifying income streams through side hustles, freelancing, rental properties, or passive income ventures, you can create multiple sources of revenue that provide stability and security in various market conditions.

Beyond investments and income streams, you can also diversify assets and liabilities to optimise your financial position. Diversifying assets involves holding a mix of liquid and illiquid assets, such as cash, stocks, real estate, and other tangible assets, to spread risk and maximise returns. Similarly, diversifying liabilities involves managing debt strategically and avoiding over-reliance on high-interest debt or single lenders. By diversifying assets and liabilities, you can optimise your financial position, reduce risk, and enhance wealth creation opportunities.

The law of diversification emphasises the importance of balancing risk and return in wealth creation. While diversification can reduce overall portfolio risk, it is essential to strike a balance between risk and return based on your financial goals, risk tolerance, and time horizon. By diversifying strategically and rebalancing portfolios regularly, you can optimise risk-adjusted returns and achieve your financial objectives with greater confidence and stability.

The law of diversification is another powerful principle in wealth creation that empowers you to spread risk, maximise opportunities, and achieve long-term financial success. By diversifying investments, income streams, assets, and liabilities, you can mitigate volatility, reduce exposure to unforeseen events, and optimise your financial position for growth and stability. As you leverage the law of diversification in your wealth creation journey, you can cultivate money wisdom, achieve financial security, and build a legacy of prosperity for generations to come. This is the kind of success that will outlive you.

The power of having multiple streams of income lies in its ability to provide financial security, flexibility, and resilience in an ever-changing world. By diversifying sources of income through various channels as discussed above, you can mitigate risks, maximise earning potential, and create a robust financial foundation. In summary, multiple streams of income not only increase cash flow but also offer protection against economic downturns, job loss, or unexpected expenses. This diversified approach to earning empowers you to pursue your passions, explore new opportunities, and achieve greater financial freedom, independence, and priceless peace of mind.

MONEY CAN MAKE OR BREAK YOU

25. MONEY CAN MAKE OR BREAK YOU

Money is a powerful tool that can make or break you, a tool that can either propel you towards financial freedom and wealth creation or lead you down a path of financial hardship and instability. In this chapter, we explore the dual nature of money and how its management and relationship with it can significantly impact your journey towards wealth creation. Money, when managed effectively, can serve as a catalyst for wealth creation. With disciplined budgeting, strategic investments, and prudent financial planning, you can leverage money to generate income, build assets, and achieve your financial goals. Money provides opportunities for growth, entrepreneurship, and financial empowerment, enabling you to create a life of abundance and prosperity.

On the other hand, money can also become a source of stress and burden when mismanaged or misused. Excessive debt, reckless spending, and poor financial decisions can lead to financial instability, anxiety, and hardship. Moreover, the pursuit of wealth at the expense of health, relationships, and personal well-being can result in a hollow and unfulfilling existence, despite material abundance. What good is money when you cannot enjoy it, and in the words of Jesus, what will it benefit a man if he gains the entire world but loses his soul. Stay alive and thrive instead.

The key to harnessing the positive potential of money lies in financial literacy and education. By understanding basic financial concepts, such as budgeting, saving, investing, and debt management, you can make informed decisions about your finances and avoid common pitfalls that lead to financial ruin.

Financial literacy empowers you to take control of your financial future, make sound financial choices, and navigate the complexities of wealth creation with confidence and wisdom.

Beyond financial literacy, cultivating a healthy relationship with money is essential for long-term wealth creation and financial well-being. This involves adopting a mindset of abundance, gratitude, and responsible stewardship of financial resources. By viewing money as a tool for achieving goals, supporting values, and creating positive impact, you can align your financial decisions with your values and aspirations, leading to greater plenty and satisfaction in life.

True wealth encompasses more than just financial prosperity. It includes physical health, emotional well-being, meaningful relationships, and a sense of purpose and fulfilment. While money is a crucial component of wealth creation, it is important to prioritise holistic well-being and balance financial pursuits with other aspects of life. By striving for balance and alignment between wealth and well-being, and achieving life-work balance, you can create a life of abundance that encompasses both material prosperity and personal well-being.

Money is a double-edged sword that can either make or break individuals in their journey towards wealth creation. By cultivating financial literacy, adopting a healthy relationship with money, and prioritising holistic well-being, you can harness the positive potential of money to achieve financial freedom and lasting prosperity. As you navigate the complexities of wealth creation, you must recognise the dual nature of money and strive to use it as a force for good in your life and the lives of others.

MONEY IS AN AMPLIFIER

26. MONEY IS AN AMPLIFIER

Money has long been regarded as a powerful force that influences people's lives, actions, and values. However, it is crucial to understand that money itself does not change a person's character; rather, it amplifies and magnifies existing traits and tendencies. In this chapter, we delve into the concept of money as an amplifier of character and explore how individuals' values, behaviours, and attitudes towards money shape their relationship with wealth creation and financial well-being.

Money serves as a reflection of your values and priorities, amplifying your attitudes and behaviours towards wealth creation. If you have a keen sense of integrity, generosity, and responsibility, money becomes a tool for positive impact and contribution to society. Conversely, those who prioritise materialism, greed, or short-term gratification may use money for self-serving purposes, leading to ethical dilemmas and moral conflicts. For example, if a psychopath suddenly came into a lot of wealth, which might just increase the chances of hurting more people, because the resources have amplified his character.

Your financial habits and mindsets are amplified by your relationship with money. If you practice prudent fiscal management, budgeting, and long-term planning, you will more than likely accumulate wealth steadily over time. In contrast, if you have poor financial habits, such as overspending, impulsive investing, or living beyond your means, you may experience financial hardship and instability despite earning significant income. Remember, it is not how much you make that matters the most, it is what you do with your increase that counts the most in this game that is the Money Game.

Money amplifies your strengths and weaknesses, highlighting areas for personal growth and development. For individuals with a strong work ethic, resilience, and enterprising spirit, money becomes a tool for realising ambitious goals and aspirations. However, those who lack discipline, self-control, or financial literacy may struggle to manage wealth effectively, leading to missed opportunities and financial setbacks.

Money has a profound impact on your lifestyle choices and relationships, amplifying both positive and negative aspects of your character. While wealth can enhance quality of life, provide security, and create opportunities for personal growth, it can also exacerbate issues related to entitlement, dependency, and social inequality. Moreover, conflicts may arise in relationships due to disparities in financial values, priorities, and attitudes towards money. There are countless stories of organisations and families who fall apart because of the love of money.

Money serves as a catalyst for personal growth and contribution when aligned with your values, purpose, and aspirations. By leveraging wealth for meaningful pursuits, such as philanthropy, social entrepreneurship, or personal development, you can amplify your positive impact on society and create a legacy of significance beyond financial success. Money is a powerful amplifier of character that reflects your values, priorities, habits, and attitudes towards wealth creation. Rather than changing a person's character, money magnifies existing traits and tendencies, revealing strengths and weaknesses, influencing lifestyle choices and relationships, and empowering personal growth and contribution. By cultivating a healthy relationship with money rooted in integrity, responsibility, and purpose, you can harness its potential as an amplifier of character to create a life of abundance, plenty, and lasting impact.

Using money to make your world a better place is not just an opportunity but a responsibility. It is about recognising the privilege and potential that financial resources afford and leveraging them to create positive impact and meaningful change in society. Whether through charitable donations, investments in socially responsible businesses, or supporting causes that align with personal values, every financial decision has the power to contribute to a better world. By prioritising purpose-driven spending and investing, you can not only improve the lives of others but also cultivate a sense of fulfilment, purpose, and interconnectedness with the global community. Ultimately, using money for good is a transformative act that not only benefits society but also enriches the lives of those who choose to wield their financial resources for positive change.

MONEY DOES NOT LIKE STAGNANCY

27. MONEY DOES NOT LIKE STAGNANCY

Money, like water, is a dynamic force that thrives on movement and activity. In the pursuit of wealth creation, the concept of putting money to work is fundamental to maximising its potential and generating sustainable financial growth. In this chapter, we explore why money does not like being stagnant and how actively deploying it in wealth creation endeavours can lead to significant financial success. Money, by its very nature, is a means of exchange and a store of value. However, money is not passive; it is a resource that has the potential to generate additional value when put to work. Like any resource, money seeks opportunities for growth and expansion, and it thrives when actively engaged in wealth creation activities. Money is not lazy; it screams for work.

One of the reasons why money does not like being stagnant is the impact of inflation. Over time, the purchasing power of money decreases due to inflation, meaning that the same amount of money buys fewer goods and services. To combat the erosion of purchasing power, you must put your money to work by investing it in assets that have the potential to outpace inflation and generate real returns.

Putting money to work is essential for harnessing the power of compound interest—a phenomenon where interest is earned on both the principal amount and the accumulated interest as already discussed in chapter eleven. By investing money in assets such as stocks, bonds, or real estate, you can leverage the compounding effect to exponentially grow your wealth over time. The longer money remains invested, the greater the potential for wealth accumulation through compound interest.

Another reason money does not like being stagnant is the importance of creating multiple streams of income. Relying solely on a lone source of income, such as a job or salary, can limit financial growth and expose you to risks such as job loss or economic downturns. By diversifying income streams through investments, entrepreneurship, or passive income sources, you can maximise your earning potential and build resilience against financial setbacks as already discussed in chapter 24.

Money thrives on opportunities for growth and expansion, and it flourishes when actively deployed in wealth creation activities. Whether it is investing in stocks, starting a business, or acquiring income-producing assets, putting money to work opens doors to new opportunities for financial growth and prosperity. By seeking out investment opportunities and entrepreneurial ventures, you can capitalise on the potential for wealth creation and achieve your financial goals.

Putting money to work is not without risks, but it allows you to mitigate risks through diversification and strategic allocation. By spreading investments across different asset classes, industries, and geographic regions, you can reduce the impact of market volatility and protect your wealth against unforeseen events. Additionally, actively managing investments allows you to adapt to changing market conditions and adjust strategies to minimise risks and maximise returns.

Ultimately, putting money to work is about taking action and actively engaging in wealth creation activities. Money is a tool that becomes more valuable when used wisely and strategically.

By taking proactive steps to invest, save, and grow wealth, you can unlock the full potential of your financial resources and achieve your long-term financial goals.

Money does not like being stagnant—it thrives when actively put to work in the creation of wealth. By harnessing the power of compound interest, creating multiple streams of income, seizing opportunities for growth and expansion, mitigating risks, and taking proactive action, you can maximise the potential of your money and achieve lasting financial success. As you embrace the concept of putting money to work, you unlock the key to building wealth and securing your financial future.

Investing your money in high-interest ventures is a strategic approach to wealth accumulation and financial growth. By allocating your funds to opportunities that offer attractive returns, you allow your money to work for you, generating additional income and potentially compounding over time. High-interest ventures can include various investment vehicles such as stocks, bonds, real estate, or other financial instruments that yield significant returns, as afore mentioned.

However, it is crucial to approach high-interest investments with careful consideration and risk management. While the potential for higher returns exists, it often comes with an increased level of risk. Diversification, thorough research, and staying informed about market conditions are essential aspects of successful investing. The key principle is to leverage your money as a tool, putting it to work in ventures that align with your financial goals and risk tolerance. This proactive approach to wealth management allows you to harness the power of compounding and accumulate wealth over the long term.

BUILD THE LIFE YOU WANT

28. BUILD THE LIFE YOU WANT

Building the life you want is a journey that encompasses not only financial success but also personal fulfilment, happiness, and well-being. In this chapter, we explore the principles and strategies for creating a life of abundance and purpose, where financial success is aligned with individual values, aspirations, and goals. The first step in building the life you want is to define your vision for success and fulfilment. Take time to reflect on your values, passions, and long-term goals in various aspects of life, including career, relationships, health, personal growth, and contribution to society. Clarifying your vision provides a roadmap for aligning financial success with your desired lifestyle and aspirations.

Once you have an unobstructed vision, set meaningful goals that align with your values and priorities. These goals should be specific, measurable, achievable, relevant, and time-bound (SMART). Whether it is achieving financial independence, pursuing a passion project, traveling the world, or making a positive impact in your community, set goals that inspire and motivate you to act.

Financial literacy is essential for building the life you want, as it empowers you to make informed decisions about money and wealth creation. Educate yourself about basic financial concepts, such as budgeting, saving, investing, debt management, and retirement planning. By understanding how money works and how to make it work for you, you can build a solid foundation for achieving your financial goals.

Living within your means is key to building the life you want, as it ensures that your lifestyle is sustainable and aligned with your financial resources. Avoid the trap of lifestyle inflation by prioritising needs over wants, practicing mindful spending, and distinguishing between short-term pleasures and long-term fulfilment. By living below your means and saving diligently, you can create financial security and flexibility to pursue your dreams.

Investing in personal growth and development is essential for building the life you want. Continuously seek opportunities for learning, self-improvement, and skill development that align with your interests and goals. Whether it is pursuing higher education, attending workshops, or seeking mentorship, invest in activities that enhance your knowledge, skills, and mindset for success.

Relationships are a cornerstone of a fulfilling life, so prioritise nurturing meaningful connections with family, friends, mentors, and like-minded individuals. Surround yourself with positive influences who support your goals and aspirations and cultivate a network of support and encouragement. Building strong relationships not only enhances your personal well-being but also opens doors to opportunities for growth and collaboration.

Building the life you want is not just about personal success; it is also about making a positive impact in the lives of others and contributing to the greater good. Find ways to give back to your community, whether through volunteering, philanthropy, or social entrepreneurship. By using your resources and skills to have influence, you not only create a meaningful legacy but also experience greater fulfilment and purpose in life.

Building the life you want is a holistic journey that integrates financial success with personal fulfilment, happiness, and purpose. By defining your vision, setting meaningful goals, cultivating financial literacy, living within your means, investing in personal growth, nurturing relationships, and giving back to society, you can create a life of abundance, plenty, and lasting impact. As you align your financial success with your deepest values and aspirations, you can build a life that reflects your truest self and brings you joy and fulfilment in every aspect.

Everything that exists is because of the invisible becoming visible as all things start with a thought. If things are done a certain way, specific results can be achieved and therefore, the first step to becoming what you want to become is to start thinking how you want to be. Develop the discipline to be consistent and hold a persistent thought long enough for it to turn into reality. The world is littered with people who quit too early before they could see any results. It is those who persevere to the end that win, if you will hold on to your belief that you can be wealthy and become all that you are meant to be. We are powerful beings capable of creating the tangible from nothing by just believing our thoughts and dwelling on them. Becoming wealthy or getting rich starts with your inner belief first. Your thought life must become greater and multiply for your physical life to also increase. You cannot expect your financial situation to change if you yourself remain the same. Your desire for wealth is the clearest indicator that you have the capacity for it. It is not evil to desire wealth as everything in life today involves the ability to afford things.

We as individuals are fully maximised when we are empowered and have the resources to acquire the necessities of life as well as enjoy being able to change other people's lives. Please know however, that you are not the only one who seeks to become wealthy as many people do so all over the world. It is amazing that only a few attain this desired wealth and it is not an accident at all. Getting rich is a specific science and comes after diligent application of the laws that govern wealth. It is not by luck or by competing with others but through the creation of your own thoughts and inventions. There is enough wealth in the world for everyone to prosper without cutting out anybody along the way. That is why, one of the most important things you can ever do is discover your true purpose and then faithfully stick to your lane. Never get afraid that will miss out to another as only you can develop and create the life that you are meant to live.

Nothing will just accidently come to you in life and though I strongly believe in miracles as does your heavenly Father, it is clear that we have a part to play in order for us to attain the life that we want: Moses had a stick, the young boy had a lunch box and even the widow had some little oil to invest. The word of God says that He will bless the work of our hands and that means we need to have some work for Him to bless. If you were to multiply God's billions or even gazillions with your zero, you will surely only get zero back. And so, it is obvious that we cannot just wish and pray for the best but must step out in faith and do something. You might be asking yourself what exactly you can do to get started and the answer lies purely in the thing that you are passionate about. So, ask yourself what it is that you would gladly do even without pay yet still find joy and satisfaction in it and therein lies your way out of poverty and lack. God in His infinite wisdom has deposited in all of us the seeds that we need to win in life. That is why He placed in all of us creative substance and even went as far as giving us an amazing mind and brain to produce faith and imagine incredible things. This makes us creative beings, so let us create.

Ask yourself what you are becoming as you go after wealth and success. This is even more important than the success that you end up accumulating because what you become is what will sustain you and keep you at the top. True happiness is not necessarily found in what you collect but in what you become. It is possible for you to have the life you want and then some. Decide today, to not only get excited about what you are learning but to get excited about this fantastic opportunity to be able to practice the wisdom contained herein. This is the main difference between the wealthy and the poor; and it is also the reason rich people look exactly like poor people physiologically and exist on the same planet.

Taking control of your own life and destiny is a profound act of empowerment and self-determination. It means recognising that you have the power to shape your own future, make choices that align with your values and aspirations, and take deliberate actions to create the life you desire. By taking ownership of your decisions, thoughts, and behaviours, you are no longer a passive bystander, but an active participant in the journey of your life. Taking control of your own life and destiny requires courage, resilience, and a willingness to embrace change. It means stepping out of your comfort zone, challenging limiting beliefs, and pushing past obstacles that stand in the way of your dreams. It involves setting clear SMART goals, creating actionable plans, and staying committed to your vision, even in the face of adversity. By taking control of my own life and destiny, you reclaim your agency and autonomy, empowering yourself to live authentically and pursue your passions with purpose and determination. It is a journey of self-discovery, growth, and transformation, where you are the author of your story and the architect of your future. Take charge of your destiny, today.

THE POWER OF PASSIVE INCOME

29. THE POWER OF PASSIVE INCOME

Passive income is a cornerstone of wealth creation, providing you with the opportunity to generate consistent revenue streams with minimal ongoing effort. In this chapter, we explore the concept of passive income and its transformative power in building long-term wealth and financial freedom. Passive income is income that is earned with minimal active involvement or effort. Unlike active income, which requires trading time for money, passive income streams continue to generate revenue even when you are not actively working. Examples of passive income sources include rental income from real estate, dividends from stocks, royalties from intellectual property, affiliate marketing, and online businesses.

Passive income enables you to diversify your income streams, reducing reliance on an only source of income and mitigating financial risk. By creating multiple streams of passive income, you can build resilience and stability in your financial portfolio, ensuring consistent cash flow regardless of economic conditions or employment status.

Passive income allows you to leverage your time and resources more effectively, maximising your earning potential and creating freedom to pursue other interests and activities. With passive income streams in place, you can achieve financial independence and escape the constraints of traditional employment, giving you more time to focus on personal growth, leisure, and fulfilment. Passive income is a powerful tool for building long-term wealth and creating a legacy of prosperity. Unlike active income, which is limited by time and effort, passive income streams have the potential to grow and compound over time, increasing in value and providing a reliable source of income for future generations.

By investing in assets that generate passive income, you can build a sustainable foundation for wealth creation and financial security. Passive income is the key to achieving financial freedom, allowing you to break free from the paycheck-to-paycheck cycle and live life on your own terms. With passive income streams covering living expenses and providing financial stability, you have the freedom to pursue your passions, travel the world, spend time with loved ones, and pursue meaningful endeavours without the constraints of financial limitations.

Passive income streams create opportunities for growth and expansion, enabling you to reinvest profits into new ventures, assets, or businesses. By continually reinvesting passive income into income-producing assets, you can accelerate wealth creation and build a portfolio of assets that generates increasing returns over time. The power of passive income in wealth creation cannot be overstated. By diversifying income streams, leveraging time and resources, building long-term wealth, achieving financial freedom, and creating opportunities for growth, passive income transforms your life and empowers you to live a life of abundance and fulfilment. As you harness the power of passive income, you can unlock your full financial potential, achieve your dreams, and create a legacy of prosperity for generations to come.

There are many reasons why you might find yourself in a situation where you have no money coming in. It could be a loss of employment, a medical condition, a family crisis, or any situation that may incapacitate you in one way or another. This is when you would wish that you had some passive income coming in. It is not too late for you to understand and harness the power of passive income, also referred to as residual income. There are always passive things that happen whether we are awake or sleeping, they are always happening in the background regardless of whatever else we are doing at the time. The greatest form of financial success is when you are no longer working for money, but money works for you. To understand how to build passive income, you need to look at your money like children and until your grandchildren have their own babies, you have not really made it. Let us break this down a little more.

What do I mean by this you might ask? When you make money, do not get all excited and spend it all expecting more money to come back in, instead, take some of that money and invest it so that it can give birth to its own children. When your financial grandchildren are born, you have one more generation to create before getting too excited so allow your grandchildren funds to also bear children and hence giving you great grandchildren. At this level, you can safely start enjoying some of your passive income even as you continue to compound it back into your financial portfolio or family. You become financially free when your passive income exceeds your cost of living. And you can get started on your journey to earning without doing any more work. Creating passive income is the best retirement plan.

Most people hate their job so much that they even dislike the road that leads up to the work building but continue going to work, day in day out because they have bills to pay. The main reason these people continue working even though they are extremely unhappy is due to fear, they hold on to the safety that a job seems to give them. Warren Buffet often says that 'we often pay too much for safety' and fear will keep you broke for a long time until you break free from it. Even when the markets are in trouble, you can still step out and create wealth. In fact, one of the best times to invest money is during a market crash. Being out of the market during a recession is the last thing you want to do because when the market is in crisis, everything goes on sale. This means that you can buy great stock at a lower price and since the market always recovers, you stand to make a fortune because you acted during a crisis.

You can start your journey towards financial freedom by learning how to stop swapping your time for money. It is possible for you to have multiple streams of income and here below are a few examples of diverse ways through which you can make money without swapping your time for it, one of them is through strategic investments. Here are two practical examples for generating passive income:

1. **Rental Properties:** Investing in rental properties is a popular way to generate passive income. By purchasing residential or commercial real estate properties, you can earn rental income from tenants. Once the property is acquired and tenants are in place, rental income continues to flow in regularly, providing a steady stream of passive income. While managing rental properties may require some initial effort, such as finding tenants and handling maintenance issues, many investors hire property management companies to manage these tasks, allowing them to enjoy truly passive income.

2. **Dividend-Paying Stocks:** Investing in dividend-paying stocks is another method of generating passive income. When you purchase shares of dividend-paying companies,

you become entitled to receive regular dividend payments, which are typically distributed quarterly or annually. Dividend income is considered passive because it requires minimal ongoing effort on the part of the investor once the stocks are purchased. Additionally, dividend-paying stocks offer the potential for capital appreciation, further enhancing the overall return on your investment.

In conclusion, the power of passive income lies in its ability to provide financial freedom, security, and flexibility, allowing you to build wealth and create a life of abundance on your own terms. By generating income streams that require minimal ongoing effort and time, passive income enables you to break free from the constraints of traditional employment, achieve greater autonomy, and pursue your passions and dreams with confidence. Whether through rental properties, dividend-paying stocks, or other passive income sources, embracing the concept of passive income empowers you to unlock your full potential, build a sustainable financial future, and live life on their own terms.

MONEY DOES NOT SEGREGATE

30. MONEY DOES NOT SEGREGATE

Money does not segregate. In the pursuit of wealth creation, it is essential to recognise that money does not segregate based on factors such as race, gender, or socio-economic background. While systemic inequalities and barriers exist, and I am no stranger to them, you have the power to overcome these obstacles and achieve financial success through determination, resilience, and strategic action. In this chapter, we explore the notion that money does not segregate and discuss strategies for breaking down barriers to success.

Despite the principle that money does not segregate, systemic inequalities and barriers persist in society, affecting your access to opportunities for wealth creation. Factors such as race, gender, socio-economic status, and educational background can impact access to resources, networks, and opportunities for financial advancement. Acknowledging these inequalities is the first step towards addressing them and creating a more equitable landscape for wealth creation.

Building wealth is a universal goal that transcends demographic boundaries. Embracing diversity and inclusion in wealth creation acknowledges the unique perspectives, experiences, and contributions of individuals from diverse backgrounds. By fostering a culture of inclusivity and equal opportunity, we can create environments where everyone has the chance to thrive and succeed financially, regardless of their background, status, colour, race, gender or identity.

While systemic barriers may exist, you have the power to leverage your personal strengths, skills, and assets to overcome obstacles and achieve financial success. By identifying your unique talents, passions, and areas of expertise, you can carve out niches in the marketplace and create value that transcends societal barriers. Additionally, leveraging personal networks and mentorship opportunities can provide valuable support and guidance on the journey to wealth creation.

Education and skill development are powerful tools for overcoming barriers to wealth creation. By investing in continuous learning, you can acquire the knowledge, skills, and qualifications necessary to succeed in your chosen field or industry. Whether through formal education, vocational training, or self-directed learning, acquiring new skills enhances your employability, income potential, and opportunities for advancement. I am probably the world's greatest champion of active learning and continuous personal development.

Building wealth requires resilience and persistence in the face of challenges and setbacks. You must cultivate a mindset of perseverance, adaptability, and determination to overcome obstacles and stay focused on your financial goals. By embracing failure as a learning opportunity and remaining resilient in the pursuit of wealth creation, you can overcome adversity and achieve long-term success.

While you can take steps to overcome barriers to wealth creation on a personal level, systemic change is also necessary to create a more equitable and inclusive society. Advocating for policies and initiatives that address systemic inequalities, promote economic empowerment, and create opportunities for all individuals to thrive is essential for creating a more level playing field for wealth creation and financial independence.

Money does not segregate based on factors such as race, gender, or socio-economic background. While systemic barriers to wealth creation exist, you have the power to overcome these obstacles through determination, resilience, and strategic action. By embracing diversity and inclusion, leveraging personal strengths and assets, pursuing education and skill development, building resilience and persistence, and advocating for systemic change, you can break down barriers to wealth creation and achieve financial success. As you harness your potential and create opportunities for yourself and others, you contribute to a more equitable and prosperous society for all.

ASSETS VS LIABILITIES

31. ASSETS VS LIABILITIES

Assets and liabilities are fundamental concepts in personal finance and wealth creation. Understanding the difference between assets and liabilities and how to leverage them effectively is essential for building long-term wealth and financial security. In this chapter, we explore the role of assets and liabilities in wealth creation and discuss strategies for optimising monetary management to achieve financial success. We will also explore a varied range of assets and liabilities in everyday life and business dealings.

Assets are resources that have economic value and can generate income or appreciate over time. Examples of assets include cash, investments, real estate, businesses, intellectual property, and valuable possessions. On the other hand, liabilities are obligations or debts that require future repayment of financial resources. Examples of liabilities include mortgages, car loans, credit card debt, student loans, and other forms of borrowing.

Assets play a crucial role in wealth creation by generating income, appreciating in value, and providing opportunities for growth and investment. Strategic asset allocation involves diversifying investments across different asset classes, such as stocks, bonds, real estate, and alternative investments, to optimize returns and manage risk. Additionally, leveraging assets through borrowing or margin accounts can amplify investment returns and accelerate wealth accumulation, although it comes with risks that must be carefully managed.

While liabilities can be used strategically to finance asset acquisition or investment opportunities, excessive debt can become a burden that hinders wealth creation. Effective liability management involves prioritising high-interest debt repayment, consolidating debts to lower interest rates, and avoiding over-leveraging that can lead to financial instability. By managing liabilities responsibly and reducing debt over time, you can improve their financial position and create a more solid foundation for wealth creation.

Wealth creation involves building a balanced portfolio of assets that generates passive income, appreciates in value, and provides financial security over the long term. This may include a mix of liquid assets for liquidity and flexibility, income-generating assets for cash flow, growth assets for long-term appreciation, and defensive assets for capital preservation. By diversifying across asset classes and aligning investments with financial goals and risk tolerance, you can build a resilient portfolio that withstands market fluctuations and generates sustainable wealth over time.

Effective wealth creation requires continuously monitoring and adjusting asset and liability management strategies in response to changing market conditions, financial goals, and life circumstances. Regularly reviewing investment portfolios, reassessing debt obligations, and adjusting asset allocations can help you stay on track towards their financial objectives and adapt to evolving financial landscapes. Assets and liabilities are integral components of wealth creation, providing opportunities for income generation, growth, and financial security.

By understanding the difference between assets and liabilities and leveraging them effectively through strategic financial management, you can optimise your financial position, build long-term wealth, and achieve financial freedom. As you prioritise asset accumulation, manage liabilities responsibly, and build a balanced portfolio aligned with your financial goals, you can create a solid foundation for wealth creation and secure a prosperous future for yourself and your family.

In conclusion, understanding the distinction between assets and liabilities is essential for achieving financial success and building lasting wealth. Assets are resources that have the potential to generate income or appreciate over time, while liabilities are obligations that require ongoing payments or decrease in value over time. By focusing on acquiring assets that generate passive income, as discussed in preceding chapters, you can strengthen your financial position and create a solid foundation for long-term prosperity. Furthermore, recognising the role of assets and liabilities in financial decision-making empowers you to make informed choices that align with your financial goals and priorities. By prioritising investments in income-producing assets and reducing or eliminating liabilities, you can increase your net worth, achieve financial independence, and enjoy greater financial security and freedom.

BAD DEBT VS GOOD DEBT

32. BAD DEBT VS GOOD DEBT

Debt is a double-edged sword in personal finance, capable of either facilitating wealth creation or leading to financial distress depending on how it is managed and utilised. In this chapter, we delve into the concepts of good debt and bad debt, explore their differences, and discuss the transformative power of good debt in building wealth. Good debt refers to debt used to finance assets or investments that have the potential to increase in value or generate income over time. Examples of good debt include mortgage loans for real estate investments, business loans for income-generating ventures, or student loans for education that leads to higher earning potential. In contrast, bad debt refers to debt incurred for consumption or non-appreciating assets, such as credit card debt for discretionary spending, high-interest consumer loans, or financing luxury items.

Good debt typically exhibits several key characteristics that distinguish it from bad debt. Firstly, good debt is used to finance assets that appreciate or generate income, providing a positive return on investment over time. Secondly, good debt often comes with lower interest rates and favourable terms compared to bad debt, making it more manageable and cost-effective. Thirdly, good debt is strategic and purposeful, aligned with long-term financial goals and wealth-building objectives.

The power of good debt lies in its ability to amplify wealth creation and accelerate financial growth when used strategically. By leveraging good debt to finance income-generating assets or investments, you can amplify returns and build wealth more rapidly than through savings alone. For example, taking out a mortgage to purchase rental properties can provide a steady stream of rental income and potential capital appreciation, leading to long-term wealth accumulation.

While good debt can be a powerful tool for wealth creation, it is essential to mitigate risks and manage debt responsibly to avoid financial pitfalls. This involves conducting thorough research and due diligence before taking on debt, assessing potential risks and returns, and ensuring that debt obligations are manageable within one's financial means. Additionally, maintaining a healthy debt-to-income ratio and having a contingency plan in place for unexpected financial challenges can help you navigate debt responsibly and protect your financial well-being.

Effective debt management involves striking a balance between leveraging good debt for wealth creation and minimising exposure to bad debt that can hinder financial progress. You should prioritise debt repayment strategies, focusing on high-interest debt first while strategically using good debt to achieve long-term financial goals. By aligning debt management with financial objectives and adopting a disciplined approach to borrowing and repayment, you can harness the power of good debt to build wealth and achieve financial freedom.

Understanding the difference between good debt and bad debt is essential for effective financial management and wealth creation. By leveraging good debt to finance income-generating assets or investments strategically, you can amplify wealth creation and accelerate financial growth over time. However, it is crucial to mitigate risks, manage debt responsibly, and strike a balance between leveraging good debt and minimising exposure to bad debt. As you harness the power of good debt and adopt prudent debt management practices, you can build a solid foundation for long-term financial success and achieve your wealth-building objectives with confidence and resilience.

LET US TALK ABOUT CREDIT CARDS

33. LETS TALK ABOUT CREDIT CARDS

Did you know that it takes 38 years to pay off a credit card with a £500 limit, if you only pay off the minimum every month? Think on that for a moment and just let it sink in. Credit cards can be powerful financial tools when used wisely, offering convenience, rewards, and benefits that can enhance wealth creation. However, misuse of credit cards can lead to debt accumulation and financial setbacks. In this chapter, we explore the best practices for utilising credit cards to maximise wealth creation while minimising risks and maximising benefits.

Before delving into strategies for wealth creation, it is essential to understand the basics of credit cards. Credit cards allow individuals to borrow money from a financial institution to make purchases, with the understanding that they will repay the borrowed amount, plus interest, later. Credit cards typically offer a grace period during which no interest is charged on purchases if the balance is paid in full by the due date.

Many credit cards offer rewards programs, cashback incentives, and other benefits that can be valuable for wealth creation. By choosing a credit card with rewards aligned with your spending habits and financial goals, you can earn points, miles, or cashback on everyday purchases. These rewards can be redeemed for travel, gift cards, statement credits, or merchandise, providing additional value and savings over time.

Responsible credit card usage is an essential component of building a positive credit history, which is crucial for wealth creation. A strong credit history can enable you to qualify for lower interest rates on loans, mortgages, and other forms of credit, saving you money over the long term. By using your credit card regularly and making timely payments in full, you can demonstrate fiscal responsibility and improve your credit score, opening opportunities for wealth-building activities.

While credit cards can offer convenience and rewards, they also carry the risk of accumulating debt if not used responsibly. To avoid falling into the trap of credit card debt, it is important to pay your balance in full and on time each month to avoid interest charges. Additionally, be mindful of your spending habits and avoid overspending or using credit cards to finance non-essential purchases that you cannot afford.

Many credit cards offer introductory offers, such as 0% APR on purchases or balance transfers for a limited period. These offers can be valuable for wealth creation if used strategically. For example, you can use a 0% APR offer to finance a large purchase without accruing interest or transfer high-interest debt to a card with a lower rate to save on interest charges. Be sure to read the terms and conditions carefully and plan to pay off the balance before the promotional period ends.

To maximise the benefits of your credit card, it is important to avoid fees and penalties that can eat into your wealth creation efforts. Be mindful of annual fees, overdue payment fees, and other charges associated with your credit card, and take steps to minimise them. Set up automatic payments or reminders to ensure you never miss a payment and avoid carrying a balance to avoid accruing interest charges.

Regularly reviewing your credit card statements and monitoring your spending activity is essential for effective credit card management. By staying vigilant and identifying any unauthorised transactions or errors promptly, you can protect yourself from fraud and ensure that your credit card usage aligns with your financial goals and objectives.

Credit cards can be valuable tools for wealth creation when used strategically and responsibly. By leveraging rewards and benefits, building a positive credit history, managing debt responsibly, utilising introductory offers, avoiding fees and penalties, and reviewing and monitoring activity regularly, you can maximise the benefits of your credit card and enhance your wealth creation efforts. As you integrate these best practices into your financial management strategy, you can leverage the power of credit cards to achieve your wealth-building goals with confidence and success.

Credit utilisation is key to healthy management of credit cards. Credit utilisation refers to the ratio of your credit card balances to your credit limits, expressed as a percentage. It is a key factor in determining your credit score and plays a significant role in your overall financial health. Understanding how credit utilisation works and managing it effectively can help you maintain a healthy credit profile and improve your financial well-being. Credit cards are valuable financial tools that offer convenience, flexibility, and rewards when used responsibly. However, it is essential to understand how credit utilisation impacts your credit score and financial stability. Here are some key points to consider regarding credit utilisation and credit cards:

1. **Impact on Credit Score:** Credit utilisation is a significant factor in credit scoring models, accounting for approximately 30% of your Score. Maintaining a low credit utilisation ratio ideally below 30%, can positively impact your credit score. High credit card balances relative to your

credit limits can indicate higher credit risk to lenders and may lower your credit score.

2. **Manageable Debt Levels:** Using credit cards responsibly involves managing your debt levels to ensure they remain within a manageable range. Avoid maxing out your credit cards or carrying high balances, as this can negatively impact your credit score and financial health.

3. **Regular Monitoring:** It is important to monitor your credit card balances regularly and keep track of your credit utilisation ratio. Aim to pay off your balances in full each month or keep them as low as possible to maintain a healthy credit utilisation ratio.

4. **Credit Card Benefits:** Despite the importance of managing credit utilisation, credit cards offer various benefits, including cashback rewards, travel perks, and purchase protection. By using credit cards responsibly and paying your balances in full each month, you can take advantage of these benefits without negatively impacting your credit score.

5. **Strategic Usage:** Strategic use of credit cards can help you optimise your credit utilisation and maximise rewards. Consider spreading your expenses across multiple credit cards to keep individual utilisation ratios low. Additionally, you can request a credit limit increase or open new credit card accounts strategically to lower your overall credit utilisation ratio.

6. **Financial Discipline:** Using credit cards responsibly requires financial discipline and responsible budgeting. Only charge what you can afford to pay off in full each

month and avoid relying on credit cards for unnecessary purchases or lifestyle expenses.

In summary, understanding credit utilisation and managing your credit cards responsibly are essential aspects of maintaining a healthy credit profile and achieving financial stability. By keeping your credit utilisation ratio low, paying your balances on time, and using credit cards strategically, you can leverage the benefits of credit cards while safeguarding your financial well-being.

REPAIRING YOUR CREDIT SCORE

34. REPAIRING YOUR CREDIT SCORE

A bad credit score can be a significant barrier to financial freedom, affecting your ability to access credit, obtain favourable loan terms, and achieve your financial goals. This is what is referred to in the world of banking and finance, as financial exclusion. Financial exclusion refers to the inability or limited ability of individuals or groups to access mainstream financial services and products offered by traditional financial institutions. It occurs when individuals are unable to participate fully in the formal financial system due to various barriers, which include but are not limited to:

1. **Limited Access to Banking Services:** Many individuals, particularly those in underserved or marginalised communities, may face challenges in accessing basic banking services such as savings accounts, checking accounts, and affordable credit options. This lack of access can hinder their ability to manage their finances effectively and participate in the broader economy.

2. **Lack of Financial Literacy:** Financial exclusion can also stem from a lack of financial education and literacy, which may prevent individuals from understanding how to access and use financial products and services effectively. Without adequate knowledge and understanding of financial concepts, individuals may struggle to make informed financial decisions and navigate the complexities of the financial system.

3. **High Fees and Costs:** Traditional financial institutions may impose high fees and costs for maintaining accounts or conducting transactions, which can disproportionately affect low-income individuals and communities. These fees can function as barriers to accessing basic financial services and contribute to financial exclusion among underserved populations especially those with a bad or low credit score.

4. **Geographical Barriers:** In some cases, geographical barriers such as the lack of physical bank branches or Automated Teller Machines (ATMs) in rural or remote areas can limit individuals' access to banking services. Without convenient access to financial institutions, individuals may face challenges in conducting basic financial transactions and accessing financial products.

5. **Discrimination and Exclusionary Practices:** Discriminatory practices and policies within the financial industry can also contribute to financial exclusion. Certain populations, such as minority groups, immigrants, and individuals with low credit scores, may face discrimination or exclusionary practices when attempting to access financial services and products at good and market-fair rates.

6. **Digital Divide:** With the increasing digitisation of financial services, the digital divide—inequitable access to technology and the internet—can exacerbate financial exclusion. Individuals who lack access to digital devices or internet connectivity may struggle to access online banking services, digital payments, and other financial tools. The most vulnerable in this category, are the elderly.

Financial exclusion has significant implications for individuals and communities, as it can perpetuate poverty, limit economic opportunities, and exacerbate social inequalities. Addressing financial exclusion requires a multifaceted approach that involves increasing access to affordable financial services, promoting financial education and literacy, reducing barriers to entry, and combating discriminatory practices within the financial industry. By promoting financial inclusion, policymakers, financial institutions, and stakeholders can work together to create a more equitable and accessible financial system that empowers individuals to achieve financial well-being.

With diligence and strategic action, it is possible to repair a poor credit score and rebuild your financial health. In this chapter, we explore the steps you can take to repair a poor credit score and set yourself on the path towards financial freedom. The first step in repairing a poor credit score is to understand the factors contributing to your low score. Obtain copies of your credit reports from all three major credit bureaus in your country of residence and review them carefully. Identify any errors, inaccuracies, or negative items dragging down your score, such as overdue payments, missed payments, collections, charge-offs, County Court Judgements, or high credit utilisation.

If you identify any errors or inaccuracies on your credit report, take steps to dispute them with the credit bureaus. Submit a formal dispute letter outlining the inaccuracies and providing any supporting documentation to substantiate your claims. The credit bureaus are required by law to investigate disputed items and correct any errors within a reasonable time.

One of the most effective ways to improve your credit score is to pay off outstanding debts, particularly past due accounts, or collections. Develop a repayment plan to address delinquent accounts systematically, starting with the accounts that are past due or in collections. Negotiate with creditors or collection agencies to settle debts for less than the full amount, if possible, but be sure to obtain written confirmation of any settlement agreements.

Credit utilisation is the ratio of your credit card balances, to your credit limits. It is a significant factor in determining your credit score. You must aim to keep your credit utilisation ratio below 30% by paying off credit card balances and avoiding maxing out your credit cards as discussed above. Consider transferring high-interest balances to cards with lower interest rates or consolidating debts with a personal loan to lower your overall credit utilisation.

Consistently making on-time payments is essential for rebuilding a poor credit score and demonstrating responsible credit management. Set up automatic payments or reminders to ensure you never miss a payment deadline and prioritise paying bills on time every month. Even one overdue payment can have a significant negative impact on your credit score, so make timely payments a top priority.

If you have difficulty qualifying for traditional credit cards or loans due to a poor credit score, consider alternative options to rebuild credit. Secured credit cards, which require a security deposit as collateral, can be a useful tool for rebuilding credit when used responsibly. Similarly, instalment loans from reputable lenders can help demonstrate your ability to manage credit responsibly and improve your credit score over time. The best place to be, is in a place of immense wealth where you have no need for access to credit, but while you work your way to your financial success, access to credit will be useful for you.

Repairing a poor credit score is a gradual process that requires patience, diligence, and commitment. Monitor your credit score regularly to track your progress and identify areas for improvement. Celebrate small victories along the way, such as paying off a debt or achieving a higher credit score milestone and stay focused on your long-term financial goals. With persistence and determination, you can repair a poor credit score and achieve financial freedom. Your credit score changes and updates every month, so a bad score today does not necessarily have to be your score the following month.

Repairing a poor credit score is a critical step towards achieving financial freedom and unlocking opportunities for wealth creation. By understanding your credit report, disputing errors, paying off outstanding debts, managing credit utilization, establishing positive payment history, and using alternative credit-building tools responsibly, you can rebuild your credit score and set yourself on the path towards a brighter financial future. As you implement these steps and stay committed to your financial goals, you can overcome the challenges of a poor credit score and achieve greater financial health and stability.

A key factor in managing your credit score is understanding and effectively utilising credit. In this chapter, we explore the concept of credit utilisation a little more, in addition to the material already discussed above. A lower credit utilisation ratio indicates that you are using a smaller portion of your available credit, which is viewed more favourably by credit scoring models. To keep your credit score healthy and support your financial freedom goals, it is essential to maintain a low credit utilisation ratio. By keeping your credit utilisation ratio low, you demonstrate financial discipline and reduce the risk of credit score fluctuations.

One of the most effective ways to manage credit utilisation and keep your credit score healthy is to pay your credit card balances in full and on time each month. By doing so, you avoid accruing interest charges and demonstrate responsible credit management to credit reporting agencies. Setting up automatic payments or reminders can help ensure you never miss a payment and maintain a positive payment history.

Another strategy for managing credit utilisation is to increase your credit limits responsibly. A higher credit limit can reduce your credit utilisation ratio, assuming your balances remain the same. However, it is important to request credit limit increases cautiously and avoid excessive credit inquiries, which can temporarily lower your credit score. While increasing your available credit can improve your credit utilization ratio, opening new credit accounts unnecessarily can have the opposite effect. Each new credit inquiry can temporarily lower your credit score, and having too many open accounts can indicate a higher risk to lenders. Only apply for new credit accounts when necessary and consider the potential impact on your credit score.

Regularly monitoring your credit report is essential for identifying errors, fraudulent activity, or discrepancies that could negatively impact your credit score. By reviewing your credit report from all major credit bureaus at least once a year, you can ensure that your credit information is accurate and take steps to address any issues promptly. While managing credit utilisation is important for maintaining a healthy credit score, it is also essential to leverage credit responsibly to support your financial growth and achieve financial freedom. Using credit strategically for investments, business opportunities, or major purchases can help you build assets and generate wealth when done thoughtfully and within your means.

Mastering credit utilisation is essential for maintaining a healthy credit score and supporting your journey towards financial freedom. By keeping your credit utilisation ratio low, paying balances in full and on time, increasing credit limits responsibly, avoiding unnecessary credit inquiries, monitoring your credit report regularly, and leveraging credit strategically for financial growth, you can maximise the benefits of credit while minimizing risks. As you integrate these strategies into your financial management approach, you can build a strong credit profile that supports your long-term financial goals and paves the way towards greater financial freedom and prosperity. Here are a few more tips and habits that will help you improve your credit score:

Know your Net Worth

Understand how much you are worth financially by writing down everything you own in terms of assets and compare them to all your debts. The difference between the two is your net worth and the idea is to move from a lower net worth to a higher one over time. This process will also give you the chance to evaluate your income and expenditure, which is vital to getting out of debt as will be shown below. Write down the result where you can see it and enjoy watching it improve with time.

Fix your Credit Score

Understand the credit scoring system and know your own score, which may not be great right now if you are in debt. But this does not mean, it must stay that way. You can improve you score significantly by knowing what items are making it bad and then making plans to pay them off one by one until they are cleared. You will notice that your credit score will begin to improve even before you finish paying off all your debts because it is based on a system that rewards effort. Every time you make a payment, your effort is registered in your favour and hence gradually increasing your score. The same is true for when you miss payments, so, make sure you stick to your payment plan.

Practice Delayed Gratification

When you get paid or receive a large amount of money, you are naturally on a high and in a great mood, but this is not the best time to go shopping as you will undoubtedly spend more than intended. Exercise self-control and resist spending your income in at least the first 2 days of getting paid. Delayed gratification also means that you do not have to have everything you want when you want it at any cost; just because your friends have it does not mean that you must have it too. Have the will power and patience to wait until you can afford it.

Eat Something Before Going Shopping

Never go shopping on an empty stomach especially when you are doing your grocery shopping. Hunger will make you spend way more than you mean to by picking up things that you do not necessary need. Eat something before you hit the shops and make sure that you have a shopping list to help you stay focused.

Detox by Changing your Habits

Identify the habits that got you into debt in the first place because if you do not change these, it is only a matter of time before you are back where you started. These habits like any other habit are now a part of who you are and happen from the subconscious. Therefore, most people who make a well-meaning conscious decision to change their lives, fail miserably because they do nothing about their subconscious and end up reverting to their hard-wired old habits.

Incorporate your Debt into a Budget

Prioritise your debt and arrange what you owe into categories that separate priority debt from non-priority debt. After doing that, make sure that one of the items on your budget is your debt. This means that you need to know exactly what you owe to budget for it. Once you have paid off some of your debt, do not hold back and start spending the extra cash with which you are left. Move the extra cash to the other remaining debt to pay it off even quicker.

Make Realistic Payment Plans

Most people get into further trouble with debt by sticking their head in the sand and avoiding their letters and phone calls from creditors. Hiding from your creditors sounds peaceful in the moment but, this only makes the situation even worse as charges are added and sometimes you will even damage your credit further by being handed a County Court Judgement by the courts. As hard as it may seem, your best way forward or out is to contact your creditors as early as you can and discuss a realistic payment plan with them. You will be amazed how many of these companies are willing to make a payment plan with you as a debt on a plan is always better than a bad debt that may never even get paid.

Do Not Get into Any Further Debt

You cannot get out of debt if you continue to accumulate even further debt, so it is understood that you need to stop borrowing more money or creating situations that put you further into debt to get ahead and become debt-free. Albert Einstein once said that "insanity is doing the same thing while expecting a different result." Remember that change is not change until you change.

Understand The Other Side of Debt

Debt collection companies buy debt off the companies that you owe at a discounted price but will still try to get usually more than your original debt by adding their own fees every chance they get. In some cases, if you offer debt collection companies a cash settlement of the percentage of the original debt, they will accept your offer because they will still make a profit since the cost for them was very low. These companies will move very quickly through the process to increase your debt if you ignore them and do nothing about it.

Consider Debt Consolidation

Debt consolidation companies are in business to make money so process will work for some people while it may leave others worse than when they started out depending on the interest rates and conditions of the arrangement. One of the advantages include having all your debts in one place and hence easy to keep track of. Debt consolidation is however simply an extension of your debt, and you are not always guaranteed a lower interest rate. It is not debt elimination or debt settlement as it is a refinanced loan with extended terms of payment.

What Help is Available?

If you need further assistance with how to deal with debt, contact the citizen's advice bureau or other organisations who will give you free and impartial advice as well as help you with useful skills such as budgeting and negotiating with your creditors.

Increase your Income

Jim Rohn always used to say that 'instead of wishing that things were easier, just get better.' So instead of wishing the price of things would go down, get wealthier! Commodity prices and the general cost of living has been on the rise for almost a hundred years now without any retreat and the chances are that this will continue to be the trend for many years to come. And while it would be nice not to have bills to pay, unfortunately, some bills will just never ever go away no matter how much you bind them. They just keep resurrecting themselves.

Have a Budget

If you want to know where your money goes, look at your bank statement. Seeing your statement will provoke you to change your spending habits and the best way to ensure that this happens is to have a budget. Make sure that your budget is arranged in important separate categories such as your mortgage, rent, utilities, insurance, groceries, fun, debt, crisis fund etc. Your financial goals will help function as a guide in your budgeting. They will help you prioritise you spending and determine what things you need to cut out of your expenditure. Anything outside your budget is something you cannot afford, so resist the temptation to adjust your budget just because you are too weak to resist the 'shiny' things and pressure from those around you or the need to fit in and keep up with social media and fashion trends. The next chapter is dedicate to learning how to put together a simple budget, which is key to your success.

LEARN SIMPLE BUDGETING

35. LEARN SIMPLE BUDGETING

Budgeting is the cornerstone of financial success and wealth creation. By effectively managing your income and expenses, you can optimise your financial resources, reduce unnecessary spending, and allocate funds towards wealth-building activities. Many of people have no clue where their money goes every month because of a lack of planning. In this chapter, we explore the importance of budgeting in wealth creation and discuss strategies for creating and sticking to a budget that supports your financial goals.

Budgeting is the process of creating a plan for how you will allocate your income to cover your expenses and achieve your financial goals. It provides a roadmap for managing your finances effectively, ensuring that you live within your means, prioritise essential expenses, and save and invest for the future. By establishing a budget, you gain greater control over your financial life and set yourself up for long-term success.

The first step in budgeting for wealth creation is to create a comprehensive budget that outlines your income, expenses, and financial goals. Start by calculating your monthly income from all sources, including salaries, bonuses, investments, and any other sources of revenue. Next, track your monthly expenses across various categories, such as housing, utilities, transportation, groceries, debt payments, entertainment, and savings.

Once you have a clear picture of your income and expenses, prioritise essential expenses that are necessary for your basic needs and financial security. These may include housing, utilities, groceries, transportation, healthcare, insurance premiums, and debt payments. Allocate a portion of your income towards these essential expenses to ensure they are covered each month before allocating funds towards discretionary spending or savings.

After covering essential expenses, identify areas where you can reduce discretionary spending and allocate funds towards savings and investment for wealth creation. Look for opportunities to cut back on non-essential expenses such as dining out, entertainment, subscription services, and impulse purchases. Allocate the savings towards building an emergency fund, paying off debt, and investing for long-term growth in assets such as stocks, bonds, real estate, or retirement accounts.

Creating a budget is only the first step; sticking to it is equally important for achieving your financial goals. Develop strategies for managing your spending and staying disciplined with your budget, such as tracking expenses regularly, using budgeting apps or tools, setting spending limits, and avoiding impulse purchases. Periodically review and adjust your budget as needed to accommodate changes in income, expenses, or financial goals.

Regularly monitor your budget and track your progress towards your financial goals. Evaluate your spending habits and identify areas where you can adjust or cut back on expenses to stay within your budget. Be flexible and willing to adjust your budget as needed to accommodate changes in your financial situation or priorities. Remember, if you did not budget for it, you cannot afford it. Part of your budget should already include a crisis fund.

As you stick to your budget and make progress towards your financial goals, take time to celebrate milestones and achievements along the way. Whether it is paying off debt, reaching a savings goal, or achieving a milestone in your investment portfolio, acknowledge your hard work and commitment to financial success. Celebrating small victories can help motivate you to stay on track and continue making progress towards your long-term wealth creation goals.

Budgeting is a fundamental tool for wealth creation, providing a roadmap for managing your finances effectively and achieving your financial goals. By creating a comprehensive budget, prioritizing essential expenses, identifying areas for savings and investment, sticking to your budget, monitoring, and adjusting as needed, and celebrating milestones along the way, you can harness the power of budgeting to build wealth and achieve financial freedom. As you commit to mastering budgeting as a foundational step towards financial success, you set yourself up for a future of abundance, security, and prosperity.

Simple Budgeting Template:

MONTHLY BUDGET

MONTH OF

INCOME

DATE	SOURCE	CATEGORY	AMOUNT

BILLS & FIXED EXPENSES

DATE	SOURCE	AMOUNT

VARIABLE EXPENSES

DATE	SOURCE	AMOUNT

SUMMARY

SOURCE	AMOUNT
INCOME	
BILLS & FIXED EXPENSES	
VARIABLE EXPENSES	
BALANCE	

DK GLOBAL COACHING

DEFEATING THE POVERTY MINDSET

36. DEFEATING THE POVERTY MINDSET

Poverty is a word most people will easily understand. And no matter what anyone tells you, poverty is never a blessing. My personal definition of a poverty mindset is the insatiable desire to always just spend for the sake of. Even when one had no plans to go to the shops or engage in online shopping, the moment money hits their account, the person with a poverty mindset makes immediate plans to spend. The poverty mindset is a set of beliefs and attitudes that limit individuals' ability to achieve financial success and create wealth. Rooted in scarcity and fear, the poverty mindset can sabotage efforts to build wealth by perpetuating negative thoughts and behaviours around money. In this chapter, we explore strategies for defeating the poverty mindset and cultivating a mindset of abundance to empower wealth creation.

The first step in overcoming the poverty mindset is to recognize its presence in your thoughts and behaviours. Common signs of the poverty mindset include feelings of scarcity, fear of failure, a focus on immediate gratification, a belief that wealth is unattainable or undeserved, and a reluctance to take risks or invest in oneself. By becoming aware of these patterns, you can begin to challenge and change them.

The antidote to the poverty mindset is the abundance mindset, which is characterised by a belief in unlimited opportunities, abundance, and prosperity. Cultivating an abundance mindset involves shifting your thoughts and beliefs around money from scarcity to abundance. Practice gratitude for what you have, focus on possibilities rather than limitations, and visualize your goals as already achieved to cultivate a mindset of abundance.

Challenge and rewrite limiting beliefs that reinforce the poverty mindset and hold you back from achieving wealth. Identify negative thoughts and beliefs around money, success, and abundance, and replace them with positive affirmations and empowering beliefs. For example, replace "I'll never be wealthy" with "I am capable of achieving financial abundance through hard work" and "It is my time to prosper, and I will succeed."

Embrace a growth mindset that views challenges and setbacks as opportunities for growth and learning rather than failures. Adopt a lifelong learning mentality and seek opportunities to expand your knowledge and skills in areas related to wealth creation, such as financial literacy, investing, entrepreneurship, and personal development. Embracing growth and learning empowers you to overcome obstacles and persist in the pursuit of wealth. When you stop learning, you become extinct.

Surround yourself with positive influences and individuals who support your journey towards wealth creation. Seek out mentors, role models, and peers who embody an abundance mindset and can provide guidance, support, and encouragement along the way. Limit exposure to negative influences, such as media or individuals who perpetuate scarcity thinking, and focus on cultivating a positive and empowering environment.

Overcoming the poverty mindset requires taking proactive steps and embracing calculated risks to pursue wealth creation. Step out of your comfort zone, act towards your goals, and be willing to embrace failure as a natural part of the learning process.

Recognise that taking risks and facing challenges are essential components of achieving success and building wealth.

Building wealth requires persistence and resilience in the face of obstacles and setbacks. Cultivate resilience by developing coping strategies for managing stress, setbacks, and disappointments. Practice self-care, maintain a positive outlook, and persevere through challenges with determination and resilience. Remember that setbacks are temporary, and success is achievable with perseverance and a positive mindset.

Defeating the poverty mindset is a transformative journey that requires commitment, self-awareness, and proactive effort. By recognizing and challenging limiting beliefs, cultivating an abundance mindset, embracing growth and learning, surrounding yourself with positivity, acting and embracing risk, and practicing persistence and resilience, you can overcome the poverty mindset and unlock your potential for wealth creation. As you shift your mindset from scarcity to abundance, you empower yourself to achieve financial success, create wealth, and live a life of abundance.

MONEY ANSWERS ALL THINGS

37. MONEY ANSWERS ALL THINGS

Money holds a central place in our lives, influencing our ability to meet our needs, pursue our aspirations, and achieve a sense of security and fulfilment. While money can unlock opportunities and provide resources for growth and development, it is essential to recognise both its significance and its limitations in the broader context of wealth creation. In this chapter, we delve into the role of money as a tool for navigating life's challenges and opportunities while acknowledging its inherent limitations.

Money serves as a means of exchange, enabling you to acquire goods and services necessary for meeting basic needs such as food, shelter, clothing, and healthcare. Having an adequate financial foundation is essential for ensuring physical well-being and security, as it provides access to essential resources and services that contribute to a comfortable and fulfilling life.

Beyond meeting basic needs, money serves as a catalyst for opportunities, empowering you to pursue your aspirations and achieve your goals. Financial resources can fund education, training, and skill development, opening doors to new career paths and professional advancement. Additionally, money can enable entrepreneurship, innovation, and investment in ventures that generate wealth and create value for society.

In many societies, money is often equated with success and status, serving as a measure of achievement and social standing. Accumulating wealth can be seen as a marker of accomplishment, providing a sense of validation and recognition for one's efforts and contributions. However, it is essential to recognise that true success encompasses more than just financial wealth and includes factors such as personal fulfilment, relationships, and well-being. Some people are so broke that all they have is money.

As valuable as money is, It is important to acknowledge its limitations in fostering lasting happiness and fulfilment. Money alone cannot buy happiness or guarantee a sense of purpose and meaning in life. Research suggests that beyond a certain threshold of income, additional wealth has diminishing returns in terms of life satisfaction and well-being. Moreover, focusing solely on the pursuit of wealth can lead to feelings of emptiness and discontentment, as true fulfilment comes from meaningful connections, personal growth, and alignment with one's values and purpose.

In the context of wealth creation, money plays a significant role as a resource for building assets, generating income, and achieving financial independence. However, true wealth encompasses more than just financial assets and includes factors such as health, relationships, personal growth, and overall well-being. By adopting a comprehensive approach to wealth creation that prioritises both financial and non-financial aspects of life, you can achieve a more balanced and fulfilling sense of abundance and well-being.

To harness the potential of money for wealth creation and well-being, it is essential to cultivate a healthy relationship with money based on conscious awareness, responsible stewardship, and alignment with one's values and goals. Practice mindful spending and saving habits, prioritise financial goals that align with your values and aspirations, and seek to use money as a tool for creating positive impact and value in your life and the lives of those around you.

Money holds considerable influence in our lives, serving as a tool for meeting needs, unlocking opportunities, and measuring success. However, it is crucial to recognise both the significance and limitations of money in the broader context of wealth creation and well-being. By adopting a comprehensive approach to wealth that prioritizes financial and non-financial aspects of life and cultivating a healthy relationship with money, individuals can achieve a more balanced and fulfilling sense of abundance and live a life of purpose and meaning.

The phrase "money is the answer to all things" reflects the significant role that financial resources play in various aspects of life. While money itself may not solve every problem, it serves as a critical tool for empowerment, providing access to opportunities, resources, and solutions that can enhance quality of life and create positive change. In this chapter, we explore the multifaceted role of money as an essential tool for addressing challenges, pursuing goals, and achieving greater fulfilment.

Money serves to access essential goods and services necessary for survival and well-being. From food, shelter, and clothing to healthcare, education, and transportation, financial resources enable you to meet your basic needs and maintain a certain standard of living. Without adequate financial means, you may struggle to access these fundamental necessities, highlighting the importance of money in addressing basic human needs.

Financial resources provide you with opportunities for advancement and mobility, enabling you to pursue education, career development, and personal growth. With money, you can invest in education and training, access professional development opportunities, and explore career paths that align with your interests and goals. Additionally, financial resources facilitate geographic mobility, allowing you to relocate for job opportunities, pursue entrepreneurial ventures, or explore new experiences and opportunities.

Money plays a crucial role in supporting health and well-being by enabling access to healthcare services, preventative care, and wellness resources. Financial resources can cover medical expenses, health insurance premiums, and out-of-pocket costs associated with healthcare, ensuring you have access to necessary treatments and interventions to maintain your health. Additionally, money can support healthy lifestyle choices, such as nutritious food, fitness memberships, and recreational activities that promote overall well-being.

Financial resources fuel innovation and problem-solving by providing funding for research, development, and entrepreneurial ventures. Money enables you and organisations to invest in innovative ideas, develop innovative technologies, and create solutions to complex challenges in various fields, including science, technology, healthcare, and sustainability. By allocating financial resources towards innovation and problem-solving initiatives, individuals and societies can drive progress, improve quality of life, and address pressing global issues.

Money serves as a powerful tool for philanthropy and social impact, enabling individuals and organisations to make positive contributions to their communities and society at large. Financial resources can support charitable giving, volunteer initiatives, and social entrepreneurship ventures that address social, environmental, and humanitarian challenges. By leveraging your wealth for philanthropic endeavours, you can create meaningful change and leave a legacy of impact and generosity. You can truly make an indelible mark on your generation.

Money contributes to personal fulfilment and enhances quality of life by providing you with the means to pursue your passions, interests, and goals. Financial resources can support leisure activities, travel experiences, personal development pursuits, and hobbies that enrich your life and contribute to your overall happiness and well-being. While money alone may not guarantee happiness, it provides the freedom and flexibility to pursue activities and experiences that bring fulfilment and joy.

And while money may not be the answer to all things, it serves as an essential tool for empowerment, problem-solving, and opportunity creation in various aspects of life. From meeting basic needs and accessing essential services to pursuing education, innovation, philanthropy, and personal fulfilment, financial resources play a critical role in enhancing quality of life and creating positive change. By recognising the value of money to empower individuals, address challenges, and pursue goals, we can harness its potential to create a more prosperous world.

THE POWER OF SELF-DEVELOPMENT

38. THE POWER OF SELF-DEVELOPMENT

Self-development is a transformative journey that empowers you to unlock your full potential, cultivate essential skills, and adopt a growth mindset conducive to wealth creation. In this chapter, we explore the profound impact of self-development on the journey towards financial success, highlighting key areas of personal growth and development that contribute to wealth creation. If you are not learning, you are not growing, and if you are not growing, then you are dying. There is no middle ground in the game of money and wealth creation.

At the heart of self-development lies the cultivation of a growth mindset, which is an attitude that embraces challenges, values effort, and sees setbacks as opportunities for growth. Individuals with a growth mindset believe in their ability to learn, adapt, and improve over time, setting the stage for continuous growth and achievement in their financial endeavours. It involves investing in education and skill development to expand knowledge, expertise, and capabilities relevant to wealth creation. This may include pursuing formal education, attending workshops and seminars, like the Transformational Seminars that I run around the world. It may also involve obtaining certifications, and engaging in continuous learning through books, podcasts, and online courses. By acquiring valuable skills and knowledge, you enhance your marketability, increase earning potential, and unlock opportunities for wealth creation.

The art of developing yourself encompasses mastering the principles of personal finance and money management, including budgeting, saving, investing, and debt management. By developing financial literacy and discipline, you can gain greater control over your finances, make informed decisions, and lay the foundation for long-term wealth accumulation. Through ongoing self-education and practice, you can navigate complex financial landscapes and optimise your financial strategies for wealth creation. It fosters an entrepreneurial mindset characterised by creativity, innovation, and a willingness to take calculated risks. Entrepreneurs continuously seek opportunities, innovate solutions to problems, and leverage their skills and resources to create value in the marketplace. By cultivating an entrepreneurial mindset, you can identify entrepreneurial opportunities, pursue business ventures, and harness your creativity and passion.

A key principle to developing yourself involves enhancing your emotional intelligence and people skills essential for success in wealth creation endeavours. Effective communication, relationship building, and conflict resolution skills are vital for navigating professional relationships, negotiating deals, and building strategic partnerships. By developing emotional intelligence, you strengthen your interpersonal relationships, inspire trust and collaboration, and create synergistic opportunities for wealth creation.

Self-development encompasses holistic personal growth and well-being, including physical, mental, and emotional wellness. Prioritising self-care, maintaining a healthy work-life balance, and cultivating resilience and mindfulness contribute to overall well-being and enhance productivity, creativity, and decision-making—all of which are essential for wealth creation. By nurturing personal growth and well-being, you sustainably enhance your capacity for success and fulfilment in your financial pursuits. You also significantly enhance your value in the marketplace. This is an ongoing journey of continual learning, growth, and adaptation to evolving circumstances and challenges. Individuals committed to self-development embrace lifelong learning, seek feedback, and adapt their strategies based on new insights and experiences. By fostering a growth mindset and a commitment to self-improvement, you position yourself to thrive in dynamic environments and capitalise on opportunities for wealth creation.

The power of self-development in wealth creation lies in its transformative ability to unlock your potential, cultivate essential skills, and foster a growth mindset conducive to success. By investing in education and skill development, mastering personal finance, cultivating an entrepreneurial mindset, enhancing emotional intelligence, prioritising personal growth and well-being, and embracing continual learning and adaptation, you can unleash your full potential and achieve financial success. As you commit to your self-development journey, you not only enhance your capacity for wealth creation but also cultivate a mindset of abundance and empowerment that transcends financial success to enrich all aspects of their lives.

The art of self-development is a lifelong journey of personal growth, discovery, and transformation. It encompasses a commitment to continuously improving yourself in various aspects of life, including but not limited to personal, professional, emotional, and spiritual growth. The pursuit of self-development involves a proactive approach to self-awareness, learning, and goal setting, as well as a willingness to challenge yourself, step out of your comfort zone, and embrace change. Key aspects of the art of self-development include:

1. **Self-awareness:** Self-development begins with self-awareness, which is the ability to introspectively examine one's thoughts, feelings, beliefs, strengths, weaknesses, and motivations. Cultivating self-awareness involves practices such as mindfulness, reflection, journaling, and seeking feedback from others. By understanding yourself more deeply, you can identify areas for growth and development. Get to know yourself better than anyone.

2. **Continuous Learning:** Self-development entails a commitment to lifelong learning and personal growth. This involves seeking out new knowledge, skills, and experiences through formal education, reading, attending workshops and seminars, and engaging in experiential learning opportunities. By expanding your knowledge and skillset, you can enhance your personal and professional capabilities and reach.

3. **Goal Setting:** Setting meaningful and achievable goals is a crucial aspect of self-development. Goals provide direction, motivation, and a sense of purpose, guiding you toward personal growth and achievement. As already discussed, effective goal setting involves setting specific, measurable, achievable, relevant, and time-bound (SMART) goals and creating action plans to work toward their attainment.

4. **Embracing Challenges:** Self-development requires a willingness to step out of your comfort zone and embrace challenges. Growth often occurs outside of your comfort zone, where you are challenged to overcome obstacles, face your fears, and push past limiting beliefs. By embracing challenges and setbacks as opportunities for

growth, you can cultivate resilience and develop new skills and perspectives. To face your fears means asking yourself what the worst thing is that can happen to you if you step out into the unknown.

5. **Personal Reflection:** Regular self-reflection is essential for self-development. Taking time to reflect on past experiences, successes, failures, and lessons learned allows you to gain insights into your own behaviour, beliefs, and values. Through personal reflection, you can identify areas for improvement, set new goals, and adjust your behaviour and mindset.

6. **Self-care:** Self-development involves prioritising self-care and well-being. This includes practices such as physical exercise, healthy eating, adequate rest, relaxation, and mindfulness activities. Taking care of your physical, emotional, and mental health is essential for fostering resilience, creativity, and overall well-being, which are foundational for personal growth and development. This is also referred to as self-love, it is impossible to love others if you are not cap able of even loving yourself.

7. **Personal Values:** Aligning personal development efforts with core values and your person al philosophy is essential for authenticity and fulfilment. By identifying and honouring personal values, such as integrity, compassion, creativity, or perseverance, you can ensure that your growth and development efforts are meaningful and aligned with your true self.

The art of self-development is a holistic and ongoing process of personal growth, discovery, and transformation. It involves cultivating self-awareness, goal setting, embracing challenges, personal reflection, self-care, and aligning with personal values. By embracing this journey, you can unlock your full potential, live authentically, and create a life of purpose, fulfilment, and meaning. I have been a champion of sticking to your own lane for most part of my life and I strongly believe that the best anyone of us can ever be, is our authentic selves.

The power of staying in your own lane lies in the ability to focus on your own goals, values, and journey without being distracted or discouraged by comparison or competition with others. It is about embracing your unique path, strengths, and purpose, and committing to personal growth and self-improvement without being swayed by external influences or societal expectations.

By staying in your own lane, you can maximise your potential and talents. When you focus on developing your strengths and skills, you unleash your full potential and create opportunities for growth and success in your own unique way, you promote personal growth and self-improvement. When you prioritise your own development and growth, you continuously challenge yourself to learn, evolve, and become the best version of yourself.

Staying in your own lane builds resilience and inner strength. When you are focused on your own journey, you are better equipped to overcome obstacles, setbacks, and challenges with grace and perseverance. This mindset also allows you to view competition in a healthy and constructive way. Instead of comparing yourself to others and feeling envious or discouraged, you see competition as an opportunity for growth, inspiration, and collaboration, which in turn fosters gratitude and contentment for what you have and where you are in your journey. Instead of constantly striving for more or comparing yourself to others, you appreciate your own progress and accomplishments, no matter how small.

In summary, the power of self-development lies in your ability to focus on your own journey, maximise your potential, and cultivate authenticity, resilience, and gratitude along the way. By embracing your unique path and committing to personal growth and self-improvement, you create a fulfilling and meaningful life that is true to yourself and your values. In the pursuit of personal growth and fulfilment, prioritising self-development over job-centric endeavours can yield profound benefits. While dedicating yourself diligently to professional tasks is essential for success, allocating time and effort toward personal growth fosters holistic well-being. Engaging in activities such as learning new skills, pursuing hobbies, or cultivating mindfulness not only enriches your life but also enhances overall effectiveness in the workplace. By nurturing personal development, you deepen self-awareness, expand capabilities, and foster resilience, ultimately leading to a more balanced and fulfilling existence. Always remember to work more on yourself than you do on your job.

HAVE A FINANCIAL PLAN

39. HAVE A FINANCIAL PLAN

Financial planning is critical to your journey to financial freedom and significant wealth creation. A financial plan serves as a roadmap for achieving financial goals and building wealth over time. It outlines strategies for managing income, expenses, investments, and assets in alignment with long-term objectives. In this chapter, we delve into the significance of having a financial plan in the creation of wealth and explore key components of an effective financial planning process. Ideas without a real plan, are simply pipe dreams.

Although I have been emphasising the significant of **setting goals**, we cannot discuss financial planning without revisiting this important skill. Financial planning begins with setting clear, specific, and measurable financial goals. These goals may include objectives such as building an emergency fund, paying off debt, saving for retirement, purchasing a home, funding education, or achieving financial independence. By identifying and prioritising financial goals, can establish a roadmap for wealth creation and align your financial decisions accordingly. To set successful financial goals, understand your passion and clarify your true value. Make sure that you are going after goals that line up with your core values and always start from where you are instead of waiting for everything to be perfect. See the end from the beginning and then work your way back to the future, this includes knowing how much wealth you wish to accumulate over a specific period. Your financial goals belong to you and are not designed to impress anyone nor for popular approval.

Before creating a financial plan, it is essential to **assess your current financial situation** comprehensively. This includes evaluating income sources, expenses, assets, liabilities, savings, investments, and insurance coverage. Understanding your financial strengths and weaknesses provides a baseline for developing strategies to improve financial health and achieve wealth creation goals.

A fundamental aspect of financial planning is **creating a budget** to manage cash flow effectively. A budget outlines expected income and expenses, allowing you to allocate funds towards essential expenses, savings, investments, and discretionary spending. By tracking income and expenses regularly and adjusting as needed, you can maintain financial discipline and maximise savings potential for wealth creation.

Debt can be a significant obstacle to wealth creation, so effective **debt management** is a crucial component of a financial plan. This involves assessing current debt levels, prioritising repayment strategies, and developing a plan to reduce or eliminate high-interest debt systematically. By minimising debt burdens and optimising debt repayment, you can free up resources to invest and build wealth over time.

An **emergency fund** is a critical component of a financial plan, providing a financial safety net to cover unexpected expenses or income disruptions. Financial experts recommend setting aside three to six months' worth of living expenses in an easily accessible savings account. These days, you can now open an easily accessible savings account with high interest, so that your money is still working for you even though it is designed for a crisis. By establishing an emergency fund, you can protect yourself from financial emergencies and maintain stability on your wealth creation journey.

Investing is a key strategy for wealth creation, and a financial plan should include a personalised investment strategy aligned with long-term financial goals and risk tolerance. This may involve diversifying investments across asset classes such as stocks, bonds, real estate, and alternative investments to maximise returns while managing risk. Regularly reviewing and adjusting investment portfolios ensures alignment with changing financial objectives and market conditions.

Retirement planning is a crucial aspect of wealth creation, ensuring you can maintain your desired lifestyle and financial independence in retirement. A financial plan should include strategies for saving and investing for retirement, estimating retirement expenses, maximising retirement account contributions, and optimising retirement income sources such as pensions and retirement savings.

Having a comprehensive financial plan is essential for wealth creation, providing a roadmap to achieve financial goals, manage resources effectively, and build long-term wealth. By setting clear financial goals, assessing current financial situation, creating a budget, managing debt, establishing an emergency fund, investing strategically, and planning for retirement, you can navigate their financial journey with confidence and achieve greater financial security and prosperity. As you commit to your financial plan and regularly review and adjust your strategies, you position yourself for success in creating and preserving wealth.

A financial plan is your way of taking stock of what you owe versus all your assets to establish your net worth, and this is the best way to track the true measure of your wealth. You do not need to wait until you have a lot of money before you can generate your financial plan. The chances are that people with no financial plan will never accumulate enough money to become wealthy because financial success is not an accident as already established. The first thing you need to do, is write down your financial statement and after putting your financial statement together, you now need to plan for your financial future. Your financial plan is the road map to your wealthy place, and you will never arrive at a destination that you do not know exists or will not even recognise when it shows up. You need to therefore, know exactly where you are going with your finances.

Make a Financial Statement

If you want to get ahead in life financially, you need to know where you are right now and then plan for your success. You cannot be believing to get out of debt for example, when you have no idea how much you owe or how much you have coming in. Your financial plan is your financial vision, it is the road map to your wealthy place, the end-game for your goals and objectives.

Sample financial goal-setting template:

DKG Coaching GOALS	Estimated Cost	Short/ Long term	Priority level	Target year
Buy a house				
Get a degree				
Pay off debts				
Buy a car				
Get married				
Go on holiday				
Start a Business				
Kids fund				
Start a charity				
Emergency Fund				
TOTAL				

Make a Balance Sheet

A balance sheet is a snapshot of your assets and your liabilities on a specific day. It is the same as taking a screenshot of your mobile phone of computer, only what is currently on your screen will show. Due to a system used in accounting called double entry, your balance sheet should always balance and hence the name balance sheet. With one glance, you should be able to see exactly what is happening with your finances, with the clarity that only a balance sheet can give you, so get one done. Here is a sample:

Sample Balance Sheet Template:

DK Coaching Balance Sheet as at 31st March 2024		
Assets		
Fixed assets		
Intangible assets		
Less depreciation		
Current assets		
Debtors		
Cash at bank		
Stock		
Total assets		
Current liabilities		
Trade creditors		
VAT payable		
Corporation Tax payable		
Net current assets		
Capital reserves		
Called up share capital		
Profit and loss reserves		
Shareholders' funds		

Write an Income Statement

Your income statement measures the performance of your business over a specified period and in most cases, it is over a year though it could be over a shorter period. Here you get to compare your revenue or income against your expenses to derive a net margin or the net profit before taxes if the taxes are not already included in the costs. Here is a sample for you:

Sample Income Statement Template:

DK Global Coaching Income Statement for period ending 31st March 2024		
Income		
Services provided		
Expenses		
Wages		
Rent/ Mortgage		
Internet & Telephone		
Utilities		
Taxes		
Insurance		
Administration costs		
Bank charges		
Travel costs		
Special events		
Net Margin		

Write a Cashflow Statement

Your cashflow statement shows you how your business has both generated and used cash as well as liquid assets over a specified period. Cash is the energy of any business, and this statement reviews the activities of your business over a longer period as compared to just one day like in the case of the balance sheet.

Sample Cashflow Statement Template:

DK Global Coaching Cashflow Statement for period ending 31st March 2024	
Opening Bank & Cash	
Bank Current Account	
Cash	
Credit Card	
Loan	
Total opening Bank & Cash	
Income	
Sales	
Payments	
Accounts Payable (Trade Creditors)	
Taxes Paid	
Loan Repayment	
Interest	
Wages	
Dividend	
Total Payments	
Closing Bank & Cash	
Bank Current Account	
Cash	
Credit Card	
Loan	
Total Closing Bank & Cash	

THE WEALTH FORMULA

40. THE WEALTH FORMULA

Achieving financial freedom is a goal shared by many individuals seeking to live life on their terms, free from financial constraints. The wealth formula serves as a blueprint for realising this goal, providing a systematic approach to wealth creation and financial independence. In this chapter, we explore the wealth formula and strategies for implementing it to attain financial freedom. The first component of the wealth formula is income generation. Increasing income streams through various sources such as employment, entrepreneurship, investments, and passive income endeavours lays the foundation for building wealth. Diversifying income sources and focusing on maximising earning potential are key strategies for increasing income and accelerating wealth accumulation.

Managing expenses is a critical aspect of the wealth formula. Controlling spending habits, prioritising needs over wants, and practicing frugality allow you to optimise your financial resources and allocate funds towards wealth-building activities. Implementing a budget, tracking expenses, and avoiding lifestyle inflation are effective strategies for managing expenses and maximising savings potential. **Saving and investing** play a significant role in the wealth formula, facilitating wealth accumulation and long-term financial growth. Setting aside a portion of income for savings and investment purposes and allocating funds towards assets that generate passive income or appreciate, are essential strategies for building wealth. Utilizing tax-advantaged accounts, diversifying investments, and adopting a disciplined approach to saving and investing are key principles of the wealth formula.

Managing debt is another crucial component of the wealth formula. Minimising high-interest debt, such as credit card debt and personal loans, and focusing on debt repayment strategies are essential for achieving financial freedom. Prioritising debt reduction, consolidating debt at lower interest rates, and avoiding unnecessary debt accumulation contribute to financial stability and accelerate wealth creation.

While you work to reduce debt, protecting assets is another integral part of the wealth formula to focus on, as you safeguard accumulated wealth and mitigate financial risks. Implementing asset protection strategies such as insurance coverage, estate planning, and legal structures, such as trusts, helps shield assets from potential liabilities and preserve wealth for future generations. Proactively addressing risks and ensuring adequate protection of assets are fundamental principles of the wealth formula. Preserving wealth is the final component of the wealth formula, ensuring long-term financial security and sustainability.

Fostering a mindset of stewardship and legacy planning ensures that accumulated wealth continues to benefit future generations. The wealth formula provides a comprehensive framework for achieving financial freedom and creating lasting wealth. By focusing on income generation, expense management, savings and investment, debt management, asset protection, and wealth preservation, you can navigate your financial journey with confidence and achieve greater financial security and independence. As you apply the principles of the wealth formula and commit to disciplined financial management, you position yourself to realise your vision of financial freedom and live life on your own terms.

Like poverty has a formula and it works regardless of who is involved. One of the biggest barriers to financial freedom is ignorance. A lot of people think that education is expensive until they realise that a lack of it costs so much more. The first thing you need to do is develop high income skills, which give you the advantage of being able to generate money without having a job or any business. This is different from a skilful job, which is limited to the industry that you work in while income skills will enable you to flourish regardless of what industry you get involved in. These are skills that you do not learn at university in an academic setting but from other successful people who are willing to pass on invaluable practical knowledge and not just volumes of memorisable information. Use your acquired skills to build a business that pays you a passive income so that even when you are no longer running around to work, your business will continue to pay you as it thrives on a system and not on your continued hard work. A passive income type of business not only makes you money but also frees up much of your time for you to apply yourself elsewhere and achieve even more. You could of course choose to take it easy, but wisdom will help you decide when the right time to rest is.

My humble advice to you is not to take your foot off the gas just yet until you have started making money from your next step of financial growth, which is investing in high return investments. Although these come with a higher risk, they also bring in higher returns. Most people fail because they invest the little money, they have by risking it all, and if they make any kind of loss, they are already out of the game before that even making any progress. The secret is to start small and start where you are, then work your way up. This process also allows you the opportunity to understand yourself better in terms of your risk appetites as well as develop better investment research skills.

Becoming wealthy is done the same way as becoming broke. All you must do, is the opposite of the other and you will get a guaranteed outcome. The wealth formula therefore can be easily expressed in two statements that are the same as they are a mirror image of each other. I like to think of it this way:

- ***Spend less than you earn = Become Wealthy***
- ***Spend more than you earn = Become Broke***

Everyone wants to attain financial freedom and yet very few people become wealthy. This is largely because success is primarily an inside job and must happen on the inside first. Your inner belief is one of the greatest assets that you possess because you were born with it and do not need to look for it or learn it from anyone. The faith that you apply is what produces your harvest, it is your belief system that affects all your outcomes and experiences. Your ability to believe against the odds is what sets you apart and enables you to see in the dark. You must believe that you can and will become wealthy before you can succeed financially. If you can see it, you can achieve anything.

Develop mastery over your tongue by taking charge of your thoughts and only speak life because your words have power to both create and destroy. Your words will always find their way back to you one way or the other and every idle word will demand your accountability someday. Make integrity your bond and be sure to keep your word regardless of who can or cannot find out about it. You may be the only one who knows the truth, but you still know about it and your own conscious will condemn you and eat away at your inner personal belief, which is key to your success. What you believe deeply will become your reality, so protect your faith with everything you have.

One of the biggest questions you will need to ask yourself on your way to the top is who you are becoming! Your personal attributes will either develop or destroy your network; you will either attract people or keep them away by how you relate to every individual. Whatever is on the inside radiates on the outside for others to see even though you may think you can hide your true feelings well. Find a way to meet the needs of the masses, discover what you can do for others and remember that whatever you move towards will also move towards you and whatever you respect will come to you.

Be enthusiastic about your dreams and always maintain a positive attitude. Knowledge is power but only when you put it to work as already pointed out in the preceding chapters. In the same way, affirmations spoken without vitality is dead weight. Learn to be flexible enough to adapt when necessary but always remain authentic and true to your original self. Stay away from unproductive chatter that leads nowhere and only spend your energy on useful conversation. Remember to laugh and have some fun, as life is too short to take yourself too seriously and to wait for everything to be perfect before you can laugh and just breathe. Give yourself permission to live your life to the full and make every day count while you still have breath.

In life, nothing just happens and that means there is a reason for everything. There is a reason some people are poor, and others are rich in the same environment; why some fail, and others succeed while living in the same country or the same city and sometimes even carrying the same last name. Those who succeed have simply employed the laws of success and have produced the results whether they meant to or not. If you find yourself on a road leading to the city of London such as the M1 and you stay on it until the end, you will get to London whether you intend to or not, it is inevitable. I can almost guarantee that after reading this precious book and implementing the knowledge inside, it is almost impossible for you to remain the same; you cannot remain broke or at the same level where you are now. "Money Wisdom and the Laws that Govern Wealth" will make a millionaire out of you guaranteed, if you will just follow through and stay on course by practicing the wisdom in encapsulated in here.

It is unfortunate that most formal education does not teach you these principles and society does not help much either by training you to conform to the system. The success of these government run systems depend on the conformity of the masses. As confusing as it may be, you will easily find people with little or no formal education in a very wealthy place with a net worth that most graduates only dream about. Most graduates end up working for these same so called 'uneducated' because the laws of wealth and riches or success exist outside the formal education system. We can therefore conclude with confidence that anyone in this wonderful world can become wealthy. Of course, there are factors that may affect diverse types of businesses just like fish will not thrive on land but will do brilliantly in water or selling electric products in a region with no electricity might prove to be somewhat of a challenge.

Most of the excuses that people use for staying broke are simply tools for the incompetent. Excuses such as a lack of capital, lack of opportunity, having no education, coming from a disadvantaged background, among others, are all factors that can be turned around and are subject to change. You are already changing most of these by investing in yourself with this precious book. Instead of complaining about what stands in the way of your success, find joy in providing solutions to some of society's problems and you will certainly find financial success and make your way to the very top of the wealth ladder. Zig Ziglar once said, *"If you can help enough people to get what they want or need, you can have everything you want or need."* Always go the extra mile by developing the habit of actively doing more than expected of you. Develop yourself more than you develop your work, find your passion, and watch the seasons of life to know when to make a move. This book is of no help to you unless you practice what you read. The mastermind principle means putting your knowledge to work and creating a fail-proof arena where you are guaranteed to win. Knowledge is key, knowledge is power, and understanding will propel you to greatness when you act on it. Wisdom is indeed the principal thing, so get wisdom, and in all your getting, get understanding.

THE SPENDING HABITS OF THE RICH AND THE POOR

41. THE SPENDING HABITS OF THE RICH AND THE POOR

A comparative analysis of the spending habits of the rich and the poor offers valuable insights into financial behaviour and its impact on wealth accumulation. While both groups may have different income levels and financial circumstances, examining their spending habits reveals distinct patterns that contribute to their respective financial outcomes. In this chapter, we explore the spending habits of the rich and the poor, highlighting key differences and lessons for improving financial well-being. Poor people buy all kinds of stuff and things, they buy with the lust of their eyes or the insecurity of trying to fit in. Poor people spend all their money as soon as it comes in and sometimes even before it comes in. When they do spend, it is mostly on liabilities before they can even consider investing any of it at all if they do get to even think of investments.

Rich people buy mostly investments and tend to invest the money before they spend on other things. Rich people buy mostly assets and not liabilities. Wealthy people have separate accounts for different things such as their taxes, their utilities, the investment etc. And rich people do not get paid into their personal account but into their business account and then pay themselves from that account. Here below are some specific key differences:

1. **Approach to Investing choices:** One notable difference in spending habits between the rich and the poor is their approach to investing in assets versus consumption of goods. The rich prioritise investing in assets that appreciate over time, such as stocks, real estate, and businesses, as a means of building wealth. In contrast, the

poor tend to focus on immediate consumption of goods and services, spending their income on non-essential items that do not contribute to long-term financial growth.

2. **Strategic Spending versus Impulsive Spending:** The rich exhibit strategic spending habits, carefully evaluating purchases and considering their long-term financial implications. They prioritise spending on investments, education, and experiences that enhance their skills, knowledge, and opportunities for wealth creation. In contrast, the poor often engage in impulsive spending, making purchases based on immediate desires or peer pressure without considering the long-term consequences on their financial well-being.

3. **Value Consciousness versus Status Consciousness:** Another key difference in spending habits is the level of value consciousness versus status consciousness displayed by the rich and the poor. The rich prioritise value-conscious spending, seeking high-quality products and services that offer long-term utility and satisfaction, even if they come with a higher price tag. In contrast, the poor may prioritize status-conscious spending, seeking to impress others or keep up with societal expectations through conspicuous consumption, often at the expense of their financial stability.

4. **Focus on Experiences versus Material Possessions:** The spending habits of the rich often reflect a focus on acquiring experiences and creating meaningful memories rather than accumulating material possessions. They invest in travel, education, and personal development

experiences that enrich their lives and contribute to personal growth and fulfilment. In contrast, the spending habits of the poor may revolve around acquiring material possessions as a symbol of success or status, despite the limited long-term value or utility they provide.

5. **Budget Consciousness versus Budget Neglect:** Budget consciousness is a common trait among the rich, who prioritise disciplined financial management and adhere to budgeting principles to achieve their financial goals. They track their income and expenses, allocate funds towards savings and investments, and regularly review their financial plans to ensure alignment with their objectives. In contrast, the poor may neglect budgeting practices, leading to overspending, debt accumulation, and financial instability.

6. **Delayed Gratification versus Instant Gratification:** The rich often demonstrate a preference for delayed gratification, delaying immediate consumption in favour of long-term financial goals and objectives. They are willing to make short-term sacrifices for long-term gain, understanding the value of patience and perseverance in wealth accumulation. In contrast, the poor may prioritise instant gratification, seeking immediate pleasure or relief from financial stress through impulsive spending, even if it undermines their long-term financial well-being.

The spending habits of the rich and the poor offer valuable insights into financial behaviour and its impact on wealth accumulation. While both groups may have different income levels and financial circumstances, examining their spending habits reveals distinct patterns that contribute to their respective financial outcomes. By understanding the differences in spending habits and adopting the mindset and behaviours of the rich, you can improve your financial well-being and work towards achieving your long-term financial goals. You must know where all your money goes by always keeping strict records. Most people wonder where their money goes because they just spend on things without any planning and without making note of it. Becoming broke is extremely easy: just spend more than you earn, and you will not even need the devil to get you broke!

Understand *the value of every pound* you have and learn how to spend each one. Never spend all your money completely, pay yourself first and do not eat your investment because if you do, poverty awaits you as there will be no harvest coming your way. There are many ways you can spend your money however, here is a proven spending formula that has worked for countless numbers of people for generations: Discipline yourself and learn to live on 70% of your earnings and you will find that you will not notice any difference over time in terms of your needs and wants. Give away 10% of your earnings to charity and invest the remaining 20% into two types of investments: active and passive capital for both your active and passive income. If you are in debt them convert your 10% of your 20% investment fund into a debt-clearance fund on every pound.

Our Lord Jesus Christ taught us to give to Caesar what belongs to Caesar and that means your taxes are a given but what you do with the remaining net will determine where you end up in life. It is remarkably simple to become poor as all you must do is make sure that you always spend more than you earn and before you know it, poverty will become your middle name. On the other hand, if you practice spending less than you earn, wealth has no choice but to hunt you down. What you keep and multiply is far more important that anything you can ever earn.

Our habits, including our spending habits are all shaped by our thinking. Both invisible and the invisible already exist and we have the power to manifest the invisible into being. The past is stored in our memory banks and memories are attached to emotions that were elicited during the original event. That is why it is normal to experience the same feelings that we felt originally when remembering a past event. The exciting thing however is that as brilliant as the human brain is, it is not capable of being able to distinguish between fact and fiction, between present reality and imagination. This means you can feed your brain with latest information and create new memory pathways to replace whatever you seek to change.

In other words, instead of reacting to life based on past experiences stored in your memory, which may even have kept you broke unto this point, you can imagine the future that you want and feed your brain with it. Take it a step further and add the feelings that you want attached to the imagined experience and your brain will respond just as though this was a real event happening in real-time. As far as your brain is concerned, your imagination is just as real as your present reality or your memories. Albert Einstein said, "Imagination *is more important that knowledge. For knowledge is limited, whereas imagination embraces the whole world."* Dare to dream and put no limit on your dreams. Dreams are free. Most adults have lost their imagination with age, the imagination that children freely enjoy.

A deeper transformation that involves the renewing of our minds, which is reprogramming our brain to think differently and produce different results, is critical for the achievement of financial success. The real transformation from poverty to riches, therefore, begins with the renewing of your mind. You are what you think, so if you think broke, you become broke and if you think rich, you become rich. You might be saying to me right now, 'easier said than done,' but I have tasted the power of the mind and of our own confession, and belief system. Together, they form your philosophy, which governs your whole life by shaping the choices that you make every day, whether consciously or otherwise. Even your lack of decision is still a decision not to act or respond and will determine your future.

Most people do not have money because their mind does not have money and until their mind is transformed, they will always be poor because both success and failure are a mindset. When you master your thinking, you become a mastermind and when you become a mastermind, you master your life and that includes your finances. Your brain is made of the conscious and the subconscious. Your conscious brain is mostly creative and makes up under 10% of your everyday life and decisions while your subconscious brain is mostly habitual and accounts for more than 90% of your everyday life and decisions. A lot of people only focus on the conscious brain and do little or nothing to improve the all-important subconscious part of the brain. To be aware of this knowledge is to be fully alive and exist in the highest possible realm of life; also known as the abundant life!

THE MINDSET OF SUCCESSFUL PEOPLE:

– SUCCESS IS AN INSIDE JOB –

42. THE MINDSET OF SUCCESSFUL PEOPLE

- SUCCESS IS AN INSIDE JOB -

Success is a mindset. The mindset of successful people plays a crucial role in their ability to create and sustain wealth. Whether they are entrepreneurs, investors, or professionals, successful individuals share common attitudes, beliefs, and behaviours that contribute to their financial success. In this chapter, we delve into the mindset of successful people in the creation of wealth, exploring key principles and practices that set them apart on their journey to financial prosperity.

1. **Abundance Mindset:** Successful people possess an abundance mindset, which is characterised by a belief in unlimited opportunities, prosperity, and possibilities. They approach life with optimism and confidence, viewing challenges as opportunities for growth and innovation. By focusing on abundance rather than scarcity, they attract opportunities, resources, and success into their lives, paving the way for wealth creation and abundance in all areas of their lives.

2. **Growth Mindset:** A growth mindset is a hallmark of successful people, who embrace learning, development, and continuous improvement as essential components of their success journey. They see setbacks and failures as opportunities for learning and growth, rather than obstacles to success. By cultivating a growth mindset, they remain adaptable, resilient, and open to new

opportunities, enabling them to overcome challenges and achieve their financial goals.

3. **Goal Orientation:** Successful people are highly purposeful, with a clear vision of their long-term financial objectives and a commitment to taking consistent action towards achieving them. They set specific, measurable, achievable, relevant, and time-bound (SMART) goals and develop actionable plans to accomplish them. By staying focused on their goals and maintaining a sense of purpose and direction, they create momentum and make progress towards their desired financial outcomes. Goal setting will show up in most of my chapters and there is no harm in revisiting these success principles.

4. **Risk Tolerance:** Successful people understand that wealth creation often involves taking calculated risks and stepping outside of their comfort zones. They have a healthy appetite for risk and are willing to take calculated risks in pursuit of their financial goals. However, they also understand the importance of risk management and employ strategies to mitigate potential downsides. By embracing risk and leveraging it to their advantage, they unlock opportunities for wealth creation and growth.

5. **Resilience and Persistence:** Resilience and persistence are essential qualities of successful people in wealth creation. They understand that achieving financial success requires perseverance, determination, and the ability to bounce back from setbacks and challenges. They maintain a positive attitude in the face of adversity, learn from their failures, and adapt their strategies to overcome obstacles.

By cultivating resilience and persistence, they stay focused on their goals and continue moving forward, even in the face of adversity. Adversity is a normal part of life.

6. **Financial Literacy:** Successful people prioritise financial literacy and education, equipping themselves with the knowledge and skills necessary to make informed financial decisions. They understand basic financial concepts such as budgeting, investing, debt management, and asset allocation, and continuously seek opportunities to expand their financial knowledge. By mastering financial literacy, they empower themselves to make smart financial choices that support their wealth creation goals.

7. **Generosity and Giving Back:** Despite their focus on wealth creation, successful people understand the importance of giving back to their communities and making a positive impact on the world. They practice generosity and philanthropy, donating their time, resources, and expertise to charitable causes and organizations. By giving back, they not only contribute to the well-being of others but also experience fulfilment and purpose beyond financial success. Giving back can be even more fulfilling than the accumulation if wealth itself.

The mindset of successful people is characterised by attitudes, beliefs, and behaviours that support their journey towards wealth creation. By cultivating an abundance mindset, embracing growth and learning, setting clear goals, tolerating risk, demonstrating resilience and persistence, prioritising financial literacy, and practicing generosity, you can adopt the mindset of success and create lasting wealth and prosperity in your life. As you align your mindset with your financial goals and take consistent action towards your objectives, you position yourself for success and fulfilment in your wealth creation journey.

Success means different things to different people. Whatever your definition of success, it is an inside job, and your prosperity starts on the inside. If you change your thinking, you will change your life forever. If your mindset is that of a competitor, move away from that thought pattern straight away and seek to create your own unique way. Your success is hidden in your uniqueness and not in your trying to be like everyone else. If you have desire mixed with focus, you can achieve anything. You already have everything you need to succeed in life as you were created to excel; we were all created with the ability to create anything we want and have exactly the life that we want and then some. The formal education system only serves to contribute to our innate ability that we already possess. Human beings are created to never be satisfied and successful people are always going after the next goal and the next milestone. It is this inner drive that moves us to greatness. Stay hungry and go after your dream with all that you have.

Anybody can succeed anywhere in the world, and the principles of success will work for anyone willing to apply them diligently and faithfully. You do not need to necessarily be 'smart' to find remarkable success, you only need to know how to operate the system and understand the principles of success. They will be hard to master at first but over time and with consistency, they will become second nature to you in your normal everyday life. Successful people set goals and focus on them until they win; they never live in the past or make excuses about why they cannot do it or why things are not working.

Successful people make decisions fast and change them very slowly, while unsuccessful people take much longer to decide and procrastinate a lot only for them to quickly change that same decision soon after. To be successful, think and act fast and then stick with your decision regardless of the challenges along the way. Challenges will always come, as the road to immense success and wealth is littered with twists and turns and many trials and tests. It is those who stick it out and persevere that get to see the fullness of their hard work and get to enjoy the bountiful harvest. These challenges are just like turbulence when flying on an aeroplane, when it comes, regardless of the intensity, there is nothing much that you can do about it but to buckle up and ride it out. Notice also, that the worst turbulence happens just after taking off the ground and when you are about to land. Both starting out and finishing strong are not easy and they will come under attack but when you have already seen the whole journey, you can rest in the confidence that your last word shall be victory. During turbulence, buckle-up and ride it out.

You cannot achieve anything in life unless you first believe it as already established. It therefore follows that successful people are all believers! You must see your dream before it can ever happen, say it to yourself long enough until you start believing it from the depth of your being. People may laugh at you at first and it may even sound outright ridiculous to you yourself but if you repeat it enough times, it will eventually sink in and take root deep inside your heart. Understand that your unconscious competence is much more dependable than your conscious self. The thoughts that we think are what become the reality that we get to see. Your thoughts are always on a higher trajectory than your present reality in the same way that success operates on a higher frequency and to achieve it, you must rise higher; you must get better for your life to get better.

Your thinking has been shaped a certain way for many years depending on how old you are as you read this book, by your environment, society, and many other factors. There is no better time than right now for you to break out of containment and away from the cycle of sameness; it is time to 'step outside the box.' The will to achieve something is what gives you the fuel and power to achieve it. The strong belief in your own belief is what creates the facts that govern your destiny. Knowing this is powerful, however, it is only effective when you act on it that the knowledge becomes a game-changer. That is why many people will get an education and learn lots of stuff but remain broke and stranded. Education means to induce, draw from within and develop a concept with understanding and not just remembering things. That is why even experience can teach you so much in life.

Successful people are disciplined and are obsessed with self-development, so they seek knowledge and new skills all the time. They read books a lot instead of spending time on their phone chatting about useless things and posting about how they are bored on social media. These days, you do not necessarily have to pick up a traditional paper book, you can download audio books and play them wherever you are, but whatever you do, read something. If you diligently follow the knowledge in this book, people may laugh at you now, but you will have the last laugh as you cannot fail! It is only a matter of time before they come back to you for help, for advice or just to thank you. As a starting point, you do not necessarily need to know how you will get it done, you just need to know that you will succeed. Believe it with all your heart and say it back to yourself; speak your dream, focus on it, and run with it all the way to the top. Imagination is the workshop where our purposes and dreams are fashioned, making your creative brain more valuable than the things that you own or can see right now.

Develop a creative brain and always seek to create new pathways. While some of the best learning is done through observation, the greatest breakthroughs are because of stepping into the darkness and producing new ideas that carry a solution to one of life's challenges. When you find the inspiration to create something new, act upon it immediately, as successful people pursue ideas that have no precedence. And when you get started, stick with your dream regardless of how hard it gets because winners are finishers, but quitters are losers as hush as this might sound. Successful people take risks and have the courage to do what has never been done before.

Successful people never quit but rather keep going regardless of what challenges they face along the way. Adversity makes you an even better man or woman! Instead of quitting, successful people always find a way out or forward until they win. Take lessons from the pushbacks of life, some of the most valuable lessons I have learnt in my life came through great adversity and were in my darkest moments where I had to learn to trust God in the dark. You win when you can turn your misadventures and failures into assets and tools for success. Going through defeat does not mean losing, it just means that you went down during some of the rounds, but it is always the last man standing that wins the fight. Make sure you make adversity pay you dividends and always reap a harvest from your most challenging times, which is how winning is done. Your strength of character is most tested when you are most challenged and not when everything is going well. Your very growth and development hinges on suffering some defeats and learning how to overturn them into victories. Success is all about finding dirty stones and polishing them into diamonds by passing them through water and through fire. Every time you go through a tough time, you have the choice to grow from the situation or sit down and cry while you feel sorry for yourself.

Successful people plan all the time and although their decision making looks instant, they mostly decide way in advance before they are ever faced with decisions to make. This is because successful people are visionaries and always see ahead even before they get started. Winning is reserved for those who can see the future before it happens, and successful people are always three to four steps ahead. Successful people see the order in the chaos; the beauty in the ashes; and the skyscraper on a construction site. And when others say it cannot be done, they scream from the inside that yes it can! This is because they have a 'can do' attitude, which is rooted in their ability to see the future in advance. If you already know that you will get to point Z from A, many things can happen between B and Y but your belief in your vision will sustain you and keep you going. This strong believe is your "why" and the size of your "why" is what stops you from admitting defeat and quitting when things get hard.

GET OUT OF THE RAT RACE

43. GET OUT OF THE RAT RACE

Society is filled with people who follow modern trends and sometimes end up being copycats as they lose their own identity. The "rat race" refers to the cycle of working tirelessly in a job or career to cover expenses, pay off debts, and maintain a certain standard of living without making considerable progress towards financial freedom. Escaping the rat race is a crucial step towards achieving wealth creation and financial independence. In this chapter, we explore strategies for breaking free from the rat race and accelerating wealth creation.

Escaping the rat race begins with **redefining success and challenging conventional notions of wealth** and achievement. Rather than equating success with a high-paying job or material possessions, individuals must prioritize financial freedom and fulfilment. By shifting their mindset to focus on long-term financial goals and personal fulfilment, you can break free from the endless pursuit of status and external validation.

One of the key strategies for escaping the rat race is **diversifying** income streams to reduce reliance on a lone source of income. This may involve pursuing side hustles, freelancing opportunities, rental income from real estate investments, or creating passive income streams through investments in stocks, bonds, or businesses. By generating multiple streams of income, you can increase your earning potential and accelerate wealth creation.

Entrepreneurship offers an alternative path out of the rat race by allowing you to build businesses and create value in the marketplace. Starting a business or entrepreneurial ventures enables you to take control of their financial destiny, leverage your skills and expertise, and unlock unlimited earning potential. By embracing entrepreneurship, you can break free from the limitations of traditional employment and create wealth on your own terms. This also allows you to completely take control of your life and shape your own destiny.

Investing is a powerful tool for escaping the rat race and achieving financial freedom. By investing in assets that generate passive income, such as dividend-paying stocks, rental properties, or royalties from intellectual property, you can build a stream of income that continues to grow over time without active involvement. Passive income provides financial stability and freedom, allowing you to break free from the cycle of trading time for money. You are not paid for your time, but for your value in the marketplace. If we were all paid for our time, everyone would be on the same salary in your organisation.

Financial education is essential for breaking free from the rat race and building long-term wealth. You must invest in your financial literacy and knowledge to understand investment principles, manage debt effectively, and make informed financial decisions. By prioritising financial education, you can develop the skills and confidence to navigate the complexities of wealth creation and achieve financial independence.

Living below or within your means is a fundamental principle for escaping the rat race and accelerating wealth creation. By adopting a frugal lifestyle, prioritising needs over wants, and avoiding unnecessary expenses, you can free up resources to save, invest, and build wealth. Budgeting is a valuable tool for managing expenses, tracking income, and optimising financial resources to achieve your financial goals.

Breaking free from the rat race requires **patience and discipline** to stay committed to long-term financial goals despite obstacles and setbacks. You must resist the temptation of instant gratification and stay focused on your vision of financial freedom. Cultivating patience and discipline allows you to make strategic financial decisions, weather market fluctuations, and stay the course on your wealth creation journey.

Escaping the rat race is a transformative journey that requires a shift in mindset, strategic planning, and disciplined action. By redefining success, creating multiple income streams, embracing entrepreneurship, investing for passive income, prioritising financial education, living below your means, and cultivating patience and discipline, you can break free from the cycle of trading time for money and accelerate your journey towards financial freedom. As you take control of their financial destiny and adopt strategies for wealth creation, you pave the way for a life of abundance, fulfilment, and financial independence.

Society has been designed to keep everyone in the same box for everything to keep spinning the right way and maintain global economic stability. It is only the few that escape this illusion of safety who break into the million flow and become the world leaders in the financial sector. We are trained to live and think a certain way starting from the first year at university all the way to buying our first home. The script is that you should get an education, buy a house and if you are the marrying type, marry and have a few kids, then spend the rest of your life paying off your mortgage and car repayments among other bills in the hope that when you retire, the pension will be enough to be able to maintain some form of sanity until we call it a day on this planet. At the centre of all this is the money game and regardless of people's opinions about it one thing is certain, one cannot fully enjoy this earthly life without it.

Most people make a big deal about how they do not need money and yet the same people get up early in the morning to go to a job they do not even like. At the end of the month, they get paid some money which they are more comfortable calling a wage because they do not want to talk about money. And in their self-righteousness, they proclaim that money is the root of all evil when in fact the Bible never says that money is evil but rather the love of it. When money owns you and rules your life, you become a slave to it instead of money working for you, which is the correct order of things. If you are anything like me, you want to help many lives financially, but at the end of the day, you can only give what you have no matter how well intentioned you are. It is almost impossible to help another person when you cannot even help yourself. You can only give what you have, period.

Is it possible to move from being poor and broke to becoming very wealthy regardless of how you started out in life or where you come from? The answer is a remarkably simple one: "Yes, it is!" Can you do this? "Yes, you can!" If you are prepared to put in the work and do what is needed, nothing will ever be able to stop you because you are the only obstacle standing in the way of your financial breakthrough. Your mindset and ignorance in matters concerning the money game is what is keeping you down and not the fact that an aunty somewhere danced over your name pronouncing some curses. Change your thinking, get understanding and put it to work and you will change your life forever. The fact that you are holding this book in your hand is clear indication that you are serious about changing your financial condition or making it better that it is now. A sign that you are determined to move to the wealthy side of life.

True success means having choice to choose and do anything you please when you want; it is defined in what you become because of your conquest. However, success is still relative, and everyone has their own version and capacity based on their own inner belief. Your capacity will determine just how far you go in life and how successful you will become. If you carry great capacity within you but settle for mediocrity, you will forever be frustrated and never be fulfilled. You will always feel like something is missing until you find your purpose and run with it. Money Wisdom and the Laws that Govern Wealth introduces you to a life of great wealth and total-life-prosperity according to the measure of your faith. By the time you close the pages of this book, you will be wealthy on the inside and the outside will have no choice but to fall in line and manifest in the visible world.

Success is not an accident as already established earlier on but a result of deliberate informed actions. There is nothing more frustrating than living below your capacity especially when you know that you deserve so much more. I have been there, and it is not nice, to say the very least. Even a car engine will complain in frustration when you are trying to go faster in a lower gear and demands that you raise your game for it to be happy. Life is very much like that, as it is in the 'biting points' of our journey to success that our true resolve is fully evaluated. It is what we do in those critical moments that determines where we end up. The choice is mostly clear, you either reduce your speed and move down to a lower level or change the gear to a higher level. I encourage you to do the latter.

Some people feel guilty about desiring to be rich but there is nothing wrong with being empowered financially, especially if you are to use your wealth for good and not just live for the money. And although money cannot make you happy, it will certainly go a long way to give you many things that are bound to make you happy such as nice food, shelter, nice clothes, cars, capital and so much more. Most of these are necessary needs of life but all require finances to achieve. Besides enjoying the good life, money will also help you empower others around you which will bring you much satisfaction and happiness. I certainly enjoy seeing other lives transformed and being part of the change.

The holy scriptures says that the love of money is the root of all evil, not money in and of itself, therefore, you are to master money and do not let it enslave you. Make money work for you because it is a faithful servant that will do whatever you command it to. It is a tool for producing and not the result. Can you be rich? "Yes, you can!" And will you be wealthy? "Yes, you will!" When your time comes to go to glory, instead of leaving lots of debt behind, be content knowing that you have left an inheritance not only for your children but for your children's children, for this is the will of God for you. Leave behind a financial legacy and pillar that will last for generations to come.

Decide today that whatever you touch will prosper and that you will leave everything you touch better than when you found it; make a mark that will never be erased. On your way to your wealthy place, consider taking out a life insurance policy that guarantees that should you die before you become wealthy enough, your family will be well looked after, and your funeral expenses will not be a burden to them either. I always insist that the best insurance policy you can ever have been the one you accumulate yourself instead of paying someone else monthly instalments over a lengthy period. So, I suggest that you only use insurance as a temporary measure until you build an inheritance portfolio of your own. Your successful investments and wealth accumulation are a more prudent form of insurance any day.

SUCCESSFUL GOAL SETTING

44. SUCCESSFUL GOAL SETTING

Successful goal-setting is a cornerstone of wealth creation and financial success. By setting clear, actionable goals, you can chart a course towards your desired financial outcomes and stay focused on achieving them. Although we have touched on goal setting in several chapters, we will look at this subject in a little more detail now. In this chapter, we explore the principles of successful goal setting and introduce the SMART criteria for setting goals that are specific, measurable, achievable, relevant, and time-bound in the context of wealth creation and financial success. Having a vision with no goals is like driving randomly without any specific destination, you will never arrive anywhere.

1. **Specific Goals:** Specificity is key when setting financial goals. Rather than vague aspirations such as "becoming wealthy," you should define precise and clearly articulated goals that outline exactly what they want to achieve. For example, a specific financial goal could be "achieving a net worth of £1 million within the next ten years" or "generating £5,000 per month in passive income from real estate investments."

2. **Measurable Goals:** Measurability is essential for tracking progress and evaluating the success of financial goals. Measurable goals are quantifiable and allow you to assess your progress over time. For instance, a measurable goal could be "increasing annual income by 20%" or "reducing credit card debt by £10,000 within one year." By establishing measurable parameters, you can monitor

your performance and adjust your strategies as needed to achieve your financial objectives.

3. **Achievable Goals:** Setting achievable goals ensures that you set yourself up for success rather than setting unrealistic expectations that may lead to frustration or disappointment. Achievable goals are challenging yet attainable within the given time and with the resources available. For example, rather than aiming to double income overnight, an achievable goal could be "increasing monthly savings by 10% over the next six months" or "earning a professional certification to qualify for a higher-paying job within two years."

4. **Relevant Goals:** Relevance is crucial when setting financial goals to ensure they align with your values, priorities, and long-term objectives. Relevant goals are meaningful and directly contribute to overall financial well-being and wealth creation. For instance, a relevant goal could be "establishing an emergency fund equivalent to six months' living expenses" or "investing in education to enhance skills and career prospects." By selecting goals that are relevant to your financial aspirations, you maintain focus and motivation throughout the goal-setting process.

5. **Time-Bound Goals:** Setting time-bound goals provides a sense of urgency and accountability, encouraging you to act and make progress towards your financial goals. Time-bound goals have specific deadlines or milestones that create a sense of urgency and help you stay on track. For example, a time-bound goal could be "paying off student loans within five years" or "saving £50,000 for a down

payment on a home within three years." By establishing clear timelines, you create a sense of urgency and momentum towards achieving your financial objectives.

Successful goal setting is a fundamental component of wealth creation and financial success, providing a roadmap for you to achieve your desired financial outcomes. By setting SMART goals that are specific, measurable, achievable, relevant, and time-bound, you can clarify your objectives, track progress, and stay focused on your journey towards financial independence and prosperity. As you apply the principles of successful goal setting to your wealth creation efforts, you empower yourself to take control of your financial destiny and achieve your long-term financial goals.

Many people have set different goals at various times of their lives and this chapter may be familiar to many of you. How is it though that most people who set goals do not actually achieve them in the end? We will consider the reasons why and see how you can set winning goals. The only way to achieve everything you want to achieve using the same time you currently have, is the setting of goals for the life you want. You can achieve anything you want regardless of your age or timing but if you refuse to set goals, you will just fumble in the dark and get nowhere. We mostly do not get anything because we do not ask. When you set goals, you are asking the questions for your success.

Take your greatest and wildest fantasies and turn them into winning goals. Everything we see was first only imagined and your goals give wings to your dream. An idea without a goal is simply a pipe dream but when your idea becomes part of your belief, it is transformed into an ideal and it is only a matter of time before you are standing in the middle of your vision. Ask yourself what you really want and how badly you want it, the begin to turn theory into tangible substance by setting corresponding goals, which can be as unrealistic as possible. It is of course good practice to set realistic goals but when you walk by faith, unrealistic goals are also just as brilliant. I, therefore, encourage you to set both type of goals and you will be amazed what you can achieve. The great Nelson Mandela once said, "it is always impossible until it is done." If all our predecessors played it safe and only set realistic goals, nothing new would have ever been discovered or created.

A goal gives you vision and if you want to achieve anything, you must first be able to see it and believe it. It allows you to give your vision a deadline and you will require discipline and consistency to get to the top. Make sure you write down your short term and long-term goals because putting them on paper or print reinforces those goals inside you and sets things in motion towards your intended result. Providence will follow you when you decide to make a move. Alongside your goals, also write down exactly what you will need to do to achieve them including the possible obstacles as well as the people who will play a role in getting you to the top. What you want to have been an action plan regardless of what you are trying to achieve and there are many types of goal-setting models including the SMART model. There is a danger in setting goals but there is even more danger in setting them without an Action Plan, so here are six things for successful goal setting or action planning that I believe will help you get started. I learnt these lessons while I was still a teenager and I still treasure them today. They are called 'the 5 Ws and the Big H'. They are simple concepts but are critical to your success:

What?

Know exactly and with as much clarity as possible what you want to achieve. Be clear about what you want even though you may not know how to fully execute your goal at this stage. You cannot afford to be vague about your vision as crowded vision is plain confusion, which leads nowhere in particular. Without a specific destination, you will take any road that presents itself and there is no telling where it will lead you. Never start a project until you can see the end first.

Why?

Your why must be bigger than anything you will ever need to do to achieve your vision. It is your why that keeps you going when the going gets tough and the darkness intensifies. People quit because their reason for doing something was too weak. Your why is your motivation and the engine that powers up your dream; it is the scale that measures your attitude, which determines how well you execute your goals. Your why is tied to your passion and purpose.

When?

Set deadlines for your goals and have specific times and dates otherwise you are just shooting in the dark. Even if you miss the deadline, make sure you always have one and always set a new one straight away should you miss the first one even though the idea is not to miss it in the first place. When you fail to set a deadline for your goals, you make procrastination your best friend and I can tell you right now that procrastination is not your friend and will ruin you.

Where?

Location is everything sometimes in business and even in life depending on what you are doing. Do your research and find the best environment for your business to thrive in. You can be successful anywhere in the world however, there are some businesses that will only thrive in specific environments.

Who?

Not everyone will come all the way to your destiny with you. Some people will play their part and move on and some you may have to love from a distance. But there are some people who are vital to the whole duration of your journey. Understand this and choose the people whom you keep close very carefully, your decision will either make or break you; it will either keep you broke or make you very prosperous.

How?

This is the strategic arm of your plan; you must map out exactly how you will practically conduct your goals and objectives to achieve your ultimate destiny. Plan everything to the last detail if you can, however, do not let this hinder you from getting started as there will be things that you will not understand right now and can learn along the way. What you can do instead is to include learning what you need to know in your goals and financial plan.

Many people do not have goals because they do not know how to set them, some do not have them because of the fear of failure and others do not have goals because they just do not understand their importance. Wondering aimlessly will not get you anywhere in life, unless you have a specific goal to target, you are not really going anywhere. If you have no direction, you will fall for anything and everything; you will become one of those people who sign up for everything going in around you and never succeed in any of them. You cannot hit a target that you cannot see no matter how good a shooter you are, neither can you do so if have a target but are facing in the wrong direction. Your goals define and clarify your purpose and purpose is what gives you meaning for living this life. Zig Ziglar said that "having money should be one of your goals and that money is not hard and cold, it is rather nice, warm and soft with nice colours." I have had both plenty and been totally broke, and I can tell you that I prefer the former.

Setting SMART Goals:

DK GLOBAL COACHING GOAL-SETTING TEMPLATE

SMART GOALS

GOAL:

S SPECIFIC	
M MEASURABLE	
A ACHIEVABLE	
R RELEVANT	
T TIME-BOUND	

E EVALUABLE **R** REWARDABLE

COACHING WORKSHEETS – SMARTER GOALS | DR DAVID KALUBA, SUCCESS COACH

Action Plan Template:

DK GLOBAL COACHING ACTION PLAN TEMPLATES

GOAL	WHY	MOTIVATION

START DATE	DEADLINE	REWARD

OBSTACLES TO OVERCOME

RESOURCES

BIG STEPS
- ☐ _____
- ☐ _____
- ☐ _____
- ☐ _____

LITTLE STEPS
- ☐ _____
- ☐ _____
- ☐ _____
- ☐ _____

NOTES

THE ART OF PRIORITISING

45. THE ART OF PRIORITISING

Prioritising is not an accident and must be done deliberately and consciously. In the pursuit of wealth creation, mastering the art of prioritising is essential for optimising resources, maximising efficiency, and achieving long-term financial success. Prioritisation involves identifying and focusing on the most important tasks, goals, and opportunities that align with financial objectives. In this chapter, we delve into the significance of prioritisation in wealth creation and explore strategies for mastering this essential skill.

1. **Setting Clear Financial Goals:** Prioritisation begins with setting clear financial goals that provide a roadmap for wealth creation. You should define specific, measurable, achievable, relevant, and time-bound goals that align with their long-term financial objectives. By clarifying priorities and identifying the most important outcomes, you can allocate resources and efforts effectively towards achieving your financial goals.

2. **Assessing Opportunities and Risks:** Effective prioritisation requires assessing opportunities and risks to determine their potential impact on wealth creation. You should evaluate investment opportunities, business ventures, and income-generating activities based on your potential returns, risks, and alignment with financial goals. By conducting thorough due diligence and risk analysis, you can prioritise opportunities that offer the greatest potential for wealth creation while mitigating risks.

3. **Identifying High-Impact Activities:** Prioritisation involves identifying high-impact activities that contribute significantly to wealth creation. You should focus on tasks and projects that have the potential to generate substantial returns on investment, whether it is increasing income, reducing expenses, or building assets. By prioritising activities that align with financial goals and offer the highest return on effort, you can optimise their wealth creation efforts.

4. **Implementing the 80/20 Rule:** The 80/20 rule, also known as the Pareto Principle, states that 80% of results come from 20% of efforts. In the context of wealth creation, this principle underscores the importance of identifying and focusing on the most impactful activities that drive most financial outcomes. By applying the 80/20 rule, you can prioritise your efforts on tasks and strategies that yield the greatest results, maximising efficiency and productivity in your wealth creation endeavours.

5. **Time Management and Productivity:** Prioritisation is intricately linked to effective time management and productivity. You should allocate time and resources according to the importance and urgency of tasks, ensuring that high-priority activities receive adequate attention and focus. By implementing time management techniques such as prioritised to-do lists, time blocking, and minimising distractions, you can optimise your productivity and accomplish more in your quest for wealth creation and financial success.

6. **Flexibility and Adaptability:** Mastering the art of prioritising requires flexibility and adaptability to respond to changing circumstances and priorities. You should regularly reassess your financial goals, market conditions, and personal circumstances to adjust your priorities accordingly. By remaining agile and adaptable, you can pivot strategies, reallocate resources, and capitalise on emerging opportunities for wealth creation.

7. **Aligning with Values and Purpose:** Effective prioritisation involves aligning financial goals and activities with personal values and purpose. You should prioritise wealth creation activities that resonate with your core values, beliefs, and aspirations. By aligning financial goals with personal values and purpose, you can find greater fulfilment and motivation in your wealth creation journey, driving sustained effort and commitment towards achieving financial success.

Mastering the art of prioritising is a foundational skill in the pursuit of wealth creation, enabling you to focus your efforts, resources, and attention on activities that align with your financial goals and objectives. By setting clear financial goals, assessing opportunities and risks, identifying high-impact activities, implementing the 80/20 rule, managing time effectively, remaining flexible and adaptable, and aligning with personal values and purpose, you can optimise your wealth creation efforts and achieve long-term financial success. As you cultivate the skill of prioritisation in your financial endeavours, you will unlock your potential to build lasting wealth and create a secure financial future for yourself and your family.

A personal favourite priority matrix that I use and live by, daily, is the Eisenhower Matrix, also known as the Urgent-Important Matrix, which is a prioritisation tool that helps me categorise tasks based on their urgency and importance. Named after former U.S. President Dwight D. Eisenhower, who famously said, "What is important is seldom urgent, and what is urgent is seldom important," this matrix enables me to identify and prioritise tasks effectively to maximise productivity and focus on what truly matters to me and my goals.

The Matrix Consists of Four Quadrants:

1. **Quadrant 1: Urgent and Important (Do Now):** Tasks in this quadrant are both urgent and important and require immediate attention. These tasks often have imminent deadlines or significant consequences if not addressed promptly. Examples include pressing deadlines, emergencies, and critical issues that demand immediate action. Make these your priority and do them now.

2. **Quadrant 2: Important but Not Urgent (Schedule):** Tasks in this quadrant are important but not time sensitive. These tasks contribute to long-term goals, personal development, and proactive planning. Examples include strategic planning, relationship building, skill development, and preventive maintenance. It is crucial to allocate time for these tasks to prevent them from becoming urgent in the future. Schedule these for later.

3. **Quadrant 3: Urgent but Not Important (Delegate):** Tasks in this quadrant are urgent but do not align with your long-term goals or priorities. These tasks are often distractions or interruptions that can derail your focus from important

objectives. Examples include unnecessary meetings, interruptions, and non-critical emails or phone calls. Other people's drama also falls in this category. Delegate or minimise these tasks to free up time for more important activities, they are time-stealers when it comes to the attainment of your main goals and objectives.

4. **Quadrant 4: Not Urgent and Not Important (Delete):** Tasks in this quadrant are neither urgent nor important and offer little value or contribution to your goals. These tasks are timewasters or distractions that should be minimised or eliminated altogether. Examples include excessive social media browsing, unnecessary social media chat groups such as WhatsApp groups, trivial activities, television, and unproductive habits. Focus your energy on more meaningful and productive tasks instead.

Using the Eisenhower Matrix allows me to prioritise tasks effectively by distinguishing between urgent and important activities. By focusing on important tasks and managing urgent tasks efficiently, you can equally enhance productivity, reduce stress, and achieve your goals with greater clarity and purpose.

BE COACHABLE

46. BE COACHABLE

Being coachable is a critical trait that can significantly impact on your journey towards wealth creation and financial success. A coachable mindset involves being open to learning, feedback, and guidance from others who possess knowledge and experience in areas relevant to your goal and in this case, relevant to wealth accumulation. As a result, in this chapter, we explore the significance of being coachable in the context of wealth creation and financial success, highlighting the benefits and strategies for cultivating a coachable mindset. Needing a coach does not necessarily mean you are not good enough. Think of any competitive field or sport, and you will find countless numbers of gifted professionals who achieve remarkable success largely because of help from a coach.

1. **Embracing a Growth Mindset:** Being coachable begins with embracing a growth mindset—a belief that intelligence, skills, and abilities can be developed through dedication and effort. Individuals with a growth mindset are open to latest ideas, seek opportunities for learning and improvement, and view challenges as opportunities for growth. By adopting a growth mindset, you become more receptive to feedback and coaching, enhancing your capacity for wealth creation and financial success.

2. **Seeking Guidance and Mentorship:** Being coachable involves seeking guidance and mentorship from individuals who have achieved success in areas relevant to wealth creation. Mentors and coaches provide valuable insights, advice, and support based on their own

experiences and expertise. By seeking out mentors and coaches who can offer guidance and accountability, you can accelerate your learning, avoid costly mistakes, and make informed decisions on your path to financial success.

3. **Actively Listening and Learning:** A coachable mindset entails actively listening and learning from others, whether it be mentors, coaches, colleagues, or experts in the field of finance and wealth creation. This involves setting aside ego, being receptive to feedback and constructive criticism, and being open to new perspectives and ideas. By actively listening and learning from others, you can gain valuable insights, expand your knowledge base, and make more informed decisions in your journey to financial success and wealth creation.

4. **Implementing Feedback and Action Plans:** Being coachable also involves implementing feedback and action plans based on guidance received from mentors and coaches. This requires a willingness to apply new knowledge and insights to your financial strategies and goals. You should be proactive in implementing feedback, setting clear action plans, and taking consistent action towards your wealth creation objectives. By translating feedback into actionable steps, you can make meaningful progress towards financial success.

5. **Embracing Continuous Improvement:** A coachable mindset entails a commitment to continuous improvement and lifelong learning. You should continuously seek opportunities to enhance your skills, knowledge, and strategies for wealth creation. This may

involve attending workshops, seminars, and training programs, reading books like this formidable book and articles on finance and investment, and staying updated on industry trends and developments. By embracing continuous improvement, you can adapt to changing circumstances, refine your financial strategies, and stay ahead in your wealth creation journey.

6. **Overcoming Resistance and Limiting Beliefs:** Being coachable requires overcoming resistance and limiting beliefs that may hinder personal growth and financial success. You should be willing to challenge your existing beliefs and mindset, embrace discomfort and uncertainty, and step outside your comfort zone in pursuit of wealth creation. By confronting and overcoming resistance and limiting beliefs, you can unlock your full potential, expand your possibilities, and achieve greater levels of success.

Being coachable is a fundamental trait that can significantly impact your ability to create wealth and achieve financial success. By implementing the tools laid down above, you can cultivate a coachable mindset that accelerates your journey towards financial independence and prosperity. As you commit to being coachable and remain open to learning and growth, you position yourself for greater success in your wealth creation endeavours.

Be coachable and stay humble because everything you desire to embark on is already out there. The chances are that somebody is already doing what you want to do or something similar. No one can make you want what you do not want, because this is a decision you must make for yourself. Once you found out your passion and what you want in life, find yourself some mentors and coaches to help you over the line. There is an ancient phrase that says, *"when the student is ready, the teacher will appear."* In the same way, you can take a horse to the water, but you cannot make him drink it. You are the reason you are not successful and nobody else. Placing blame on others will only paralyse you.

When you find a coach, your goal is not to impress and show off how good you are. This is the time for you to talk less and listen more; it is time for you to learn and not prove your worth. Being coachable means being teachable and this also means accepting that you do not know everything. Even the most talented people in the world need a coach, so finding a coach is not in any way an indication that you are not talented or good enough. Brilliant athletes all over the world have always needed a coach from the best golfers to the best footballers in the world. Your reading of this book is evidence that you are willing to learn and are ready to be a student and sharpen your brilliance.

One of my most favourite role models of our time, Bruce Lee explains this subject in a very distinct and straightforward way by demonstrating it using two glasses, one containing coke and the other clear water. He would then go on to show that until the student empties their glass of coke, there is no room for his clear glass of water, which represented the knowledge that he possessed and was willing to pass on. He went on to explain that once you were prepared to let go of what you think you know; only then will you be ready for him to collaborate with you. By this, he did not mean that everything you knew was useless but only that you were prepared to take on latest information and learn new skills. You cannot really do much with a full cup until you create more room for new content.

Bruce Lee would go on to talk about how you should be to succeed in life by likening attitude to water. He would say, "Empty your mind. Be formless. Shapeless like water. When you put water in a cup, it becomes the cup. If you put water in a bottle, it becomes the bottle. If you put water in a tea pot, it becomes the tea pot. Now water can flow, or it can crash, be water my friend." I like this analogy as it sums up the attitude of someone who is ready to learn and is fully coachable. Being coachable is like a field getting ready for seed, until it is ready and open to receive seed, it does not matter how good that seed is, there will be no growth in that field. Therefore, a farmer would never scatter seed onto concrete as he knows that the ground is not suitable for farming. I will never stop learning no matter how old I get because there is always something new to learn in life. In fact, life is so amazing, just when you think you have got it all figured out, it will create brand new questions that you have no answers to.

UNDERSTANDING THE LANGUAGE OF WEALTH AND MONEY

47. UNDERSTANDING THE LANGUAGE OF WEALTH AND MONEY

Understanding the language of wealth and money is essential for anyone seeking to navigate the complexities of financial markets, investments, and wealth creation strategies. Like learning a new language, mastering the vocabulary, concepts, and principles of finance empowers you to make informed decisions and effectively manage your financial affairs. In this chapter, we delve into the language of wealth and money, exploring key terms, concepts, and principles that are fundamental to financial literacy and success.

Financial Literacy: Financial literacy is the foundation of understanding the language of wealth and money. It encompasses the knowledge and skills necessary to make informed financial decisions, manage personal finances, and navigate the complexities of the financial system. Financial literacy includes understanding concepts such as budgeting, saving, investing, debt management, risk management, and retirement planning. By enhancing financial literacy, you can improve your financial well-being and make sound decisions to achieve your wealth creation goals.

Key Financial Terms and Concepts: To understand the language of wealth and money, you must familiarise yourself with key financial terms and concepts. This includes terms related to investments financial instruments, asset classes, financial statements, and economic indicators. By mastering these terms and concepts, you can effectively communicate and make informed decisions in the financial realm.

Principles of Wealth Creation: Understanding the principles of wealth creation is essential for individuals seeking to build and preserve wealth over the long term. These principles include concepts such as compounding, diversification, risk management, asset allocation, and time value of money. By applying these principles, you can optimise your investment strategies, minimise risks, and maximise returns on your wealth creation journey.

Investment Strategies and Vehicles: The language of wealth and money also encompasses various investment strategies and vehicles available to investors. This includes strategies such as value investing, growth investing, income investing, and passive investing, as well as investment vehicles such as stocks, bonds, real estate, mutual funds, ETFs, and alternative investments. Understanding the characteristics, risks, and potential returns of different investment strategies and vehicles empowers you to make informed investment decisions aligned with your financial goals and risk tolerance.

Financial Planning and Management: Financial planning and management are integral components of the language of wealth and money. This includes creating financial plans, setting financial goals, budgeting, saving, debt management, retirement planning, tax planning, estate planning, and insurance planning. By developing comprehensive financial plans and implementing sound financial management practices, you can achieve financial security, build wealth, and achieve your long-term objectives.

Economic and Market Trends: Understanding economic and market trends is essential for individuals seeking to navigate financial markets and make informed investment decisions. This includes staying updated on macroeconomic indicators, geopolitical events, market trends, industry developments, and regulatory changes that may impact financial markets and investment opportunities. By staying informed and proactive, you can capitalise on opportunities and mitigate risks in ever-changing financial landscapes.

Mastering the language of wealth and money is a fundamental step towards achieving financial literacy and success. By familiarising yourself with key financial terms, concepts, principles, investment strategies, and economic trends, you can enhance your financial literacy, make informed decisions, and effectively manage your financial affairs. As you commit to continuous learning and improvement in understanding the language of wealth and money, you empower yourself to achieve financial security, build wealth, and create a prosperous future.

The love of money is the root of all evil and yet money answers all things. If you cannot speak a certain language, the chances are that you will always get what is being said wrong or you will not even understand anything depending on how little you understand. In the same way, most people mess up in their finances simply because they do not understand the unique language of money. Money does not have value but is a tool that is used to transmit value.

In the past, when money was in the form of tangible gold or silver, it had value itself. Money is only symbolic and most of the time, you never even get to see it except on your screen in digital print. Understanding the money language will set you apart because you will not only be able to speak the language but also take control of the realm of money. The world of finance has a large vocabulary and I encourage you to learn what most of the language means. Let us look at a few carefully selected useful financial terms that will help you understand money better:

1. **Assets:**

    Resources owned by an individual or entity that have economic value and can be converted into cash. Examples are cash, investments, property, and equipment.

2. **Liabilities:**

    Financial obligations or debts owed by an individual or entity to external parties. Liabilities include loans, mortgages, accounts payable, and other expenses.

3. **Equity:**

    The value of an individual's or entity's ownership interest in assets after deducting liabilities. It represents the residual interest in assets after all debts and obligations have been paid off.

4. **Income:**

    The amount of money earned or received by an individual or entity from various sources, including wages, salaries, interest, dividends, rental income, and profits.

5. **Expenses:**

    Costs incurred by an individual or entity in the process of generating income or conducting business operations.

Expenses include rent, utilities, salaries, supplies, transport, research, advertising and taxes.

6. **Profit:**

    The financial gain or excess of income over expenses generated by an individual or entity during a specific period. Profit indicates the financial performance and profitability of a business or investment.

7. **Revenue:**

    The total income generated by an individual or entity from the sale of goods, provision of services, or other business activities before deducting expenses.

8. **Cost of Goods Sold (COGS):**

    The direct costs associated with producing or purchasing the goods sold by a business. COGS includes expenses such as raw materials, labour, and manufacturing overhead.

9. **Gross Profit:**

    The difference between revenue and the cost of goods sold. Gross profit represents the profitability of a business's core operations before deducting expenses for your business operations.

10. **Net Profit:**

    The profit remaining after deducting all expenses, including operating expenses, taxes, interest, and depreciation, from total revenue. Net profit reflects the overall profitability of a business or investment.

11. **Cash Flow:**

    The movement of cash in and out of a business or individual's accounts during a specific period. Positive cash flow occurs when cash inflows exceed cash outflows, while negative cash flow occurs when cash outflows exceed cash inflows. It goes without saying which type is better.

12. **Balance Sheet:**

    A financial statement that provides a snapshot of an individual's or entity's financial position at a specific point in time. The balance sheet summarises assets, liabilities, and equity, showing the net worth of the entity.

13. **Income Statement:**

    A financial statement that reports an individual's or entity's financial performance over a specific period. The income statement summarises revenue, expenses, and profit or loss generated during the period.

14. **Cash Flow Statement:**

    A financial statement that provides an overview of an individual's or entity's cash inflows and outflows during a specific period. The cash flow statement categorises cash flows into operating, investing, and financing activities.

15. **Return on Investment (ROI):**

    A financial metric used to evaluate the profitability of an investment relative to its cost. ROI is calculated by dividing the net profit or gain from the investment by the initial investment cost and expressing the result as a percentage.

16. **Interest:**

The cost of borrowing money or the return earned on savings or investments. Interest is typically expressed as a percentage of the principal amount and is paid or received over a specified period.

17. **Depreciation:**

The gradual decrease in the value of an asset over time due to wear and tear, obsolescence, or other factors. Depreciation is recorded as an expense on the income statement and reduces the asset's book value on the balance sheet.

18. **Amortization:**

The process of spreading the cost of an intangible asset, such as a loan or patent, over its useful life. Amortization is recorded as an expense on the income statement and reduces the asset's book value on the balance sheet.

19. **Dividend:**

A distribution of profits or earnings paid to shareholders of a corporation as a return on their investment. Dividends are typically paid in cash or additional shares of stock and are declared by the company's board of directors.

20. **Capital:**

Financial resources or funds used by an individual or entity to invest in assets, conduct business operations, or generate income. Capital can include equity capital (ownership stake) and debt capital (borrowed funds).

21. **Credit score**:

This is the number that financial institutions such as banks use to measure your ability to repay money borrowed from them. It is a system that different companies use to report financial behaviour into a collective database both for individuals as well as companies.

22. **Credit:**

This is the ability to borrow money and will go up and down based on your financial behaviour or practices. Credit can also mean that your bank account has money which is yours and is above zero in terms of your bank balance or a financial transaction.

23. **Debit:**

This refers to a form of deduction that means that either money is being taken away from you or you have gone over zero and into minus on your bank balance.

24. **Asset allocation**:

This is when you choose the proportion of your investment portfolio that you would like, to different asset classes in line with your own risk appetite and tolerance as well as personal goals.

25. **Debt**:

This is when you used your credit to borrow money and now you owe someone or a company an amount of money, which needs to be paid back over an agreed period. In chapter 32, we deal with bad and good debt.

26. **Stocks and Shares**:

Stocks are the same as shares and they represent ownership in a company or business. By buying a piece of a company, you become a shareholder and become entitled to that company's earnings referred to as dividends. You do not have to buy the whole company.

27. **Bonds**:

Bonds are fixed income securities and are debt investments, meaning you lend money to the government or an organisation, over a specified period at a fixed interest rate. You would then receive the matured amount at the end of the agreed term after having received periodic interest payments throughout the tenure. There are other types of bonds such as premium bonds. These are bonds which are issued by National Savings and Investment (NS&I) and are designed around a prize draw system where investors can earn anything between pounds and a million pounds, all of which is totally tax free.

28. **Financial or fiscal year**:

   This refers to a year as stipulated for accounting or taxing purposes for the company and the government respectively and may not be the same as the calendar year.

29. **Capital Gains**:

   This refers to the growth in the value of your investment or assets beyond the original or initial value. The opposite of this is a loss, which would be referred to as a capital loss because the value of your investment has dropped below the purchase price.

30. **Escrow**:

   This is when an impartial party holds an account on behalf of two parties involved in a transaction and the funds remain untouched until the terms of the contract are fulfilled. Most business will use a law firm for this purpose.

31. **Annuity**:

   This is a retirement package sold by insurance companies to provide the benefit of tax deferral while still protecting the principle. It can either work for you or against you depending on its cost.

32. **Interest rate**:

   This is the proportion of borrowed funds that is charged on a loan and is normally expressed an annual percentage of the outstanding amount.

33. **Compound interest**:

Compound interest can mean two different things depending on whether you are the borrower or the investor. If you are the borrower, it is the interest charged on the original amount that you have borrowed including the interest added over the duration of the loan. However, if you are saving or investing, it is the interest that you earn on the amount deposited including the interest added over the duration of your investment.

34. **Net worth**:

This is the difference between your assets and your liabilities and can be calculated by adding up the total value of your assets including cash at the bank and then subtracting all your debt. The result is your net worth, and it is important that you know yours.

35. **Premium**:

These are payments that you make to your insurance company in exchange for protection from possible financial losses as stipulated in your insurance policy.

36. **Break-even**:

This is when a company or business reaches a point of balance in its operation when the profits are equivalent to the costs and there is neither profit nor loss. It is always good practice to know in advance when you might hit this goal in your business even before you get started because this is what determines when you will start making a profit from the business.

37. **Credit score**:
    This is the number that financial institutions such as banks use to measure your ability to repay money borrowed from them. It is a system that different companies use to report financial behaviour into a collective database both for individuals as well as companies.

These are just a few key financial terms and their definitions and are by no means exhaustive. The field of finance encompasses a wide range of concepts and terminology, each playing a crucial role in understanding and managing financial matters effectively.

UNDERSTANDING INVESTMENTS

48. UNDERSTANDING INVESTMENTS

Successful investing is a cornerstone of wealth creation, allowing individuals to grow their assets over time through strategic allocation of capital. Whether investing in stocks, bonds, real estate, or other asset classes, understanding the principles of successful investing is essential for achieving long-term financial goals. In this chapter, we explore the strategies, principles, and best practices of successful investing in the creation of wealth.

Goal Alignment: Successful investing begins with aligning investment strategies with financial goals. You must clarify your investment objectives, whether it is generating passive income, preserving capital, or achieving long-term growth. By defining clear investment goals and time horizons, you can tailor your investment strategies to meet your specific financial objectives.

Risk Management: Effective risk management is crucial in successful investing. You must assess your risk tolerance and diversify your investment portfolio to minimise exposure to market volatility. Diversification across asset classes, industries, and geographic regions can help spread risk and reduce the impact of market downturns on investment returns. Additionally, you should conduct thorough due diligence and research before making investment decisions to mitigate potential risks.

Asset Allocation: Asset allocation is a key determinant of investment success. By strategically allocating capital across different asset classes, such as stocks, bonds, real estate, and alternative investments, you can optimise your risk-return profile. The appropriate asset allocation depends on factors such as investment objectives, risk tolerance, time horizon, and market conditions. Rebalancing the investment portfolio periodically to maintain the desired asset allocation is essential for long-term wealth creation.

Long-Term Perspective: Successful investors adopt a long-term perspective when making investment decisions. They understand that short-term market fluctuations are inevitable and focus on the fundamentals of the investment rather than reacting to short-term volatility. By staying disciplined and patient during market downturns, you can capitalise on buying opportunities and benefit from the power of compounding over time.

Fundamental Analysis: Fundamental analysis is a fundamental principle of successful investing, especially in equity markets. You must analyse the underlying financial health, performance, and growth prospects of companies before making investment decisions. Factors such as revenue growth, earnings potential, cash flow, profitability, competitive positioning, and management quality must be evaluated to assess the intrinsic value of the investment. By conducting thorough fundamental analysis, you can make informed investment decisions based on the underlying fundamentals of the asset.

Portfolio Monitoring and Rebalancing: To be a successful investor, you must regularly monitor your investment portfolio and rebalance it as needed to maintain the desired asset allocation. You must review investment performance, assess portfolio diversification, and adjust investment strategies based on changing market conditions and investment objectives. By actively managing your investment portfolio, you can optimise returns, minimise risks, and stay on track towards achieving your financial goals.

Continuous Learning and Adaptation: Successful investing requires a commitment to continuous learning and adaptation. You must stay informed about market trends, economic developments, and industry dynamics through research, financial news, and professional networks. Remain open to new investment opportunities and adapt your investment strategies based on evolving market conditions and emerging trends. By staying proactive and flexible, you can capitalise on opportunities and navigate challenges in the dynamic investment landscape.

Successful investing is a fundamental pillar of wealth creation, enabling you to achieve your financial goals and build long-term wealth. By aligning your investment strategies with financial your objectives, managing risks, diversifying portfolios, maintaining a long-term perspective, conducting fundamental analysis, monitoring portfolios, and continuously learning and adapting, you can enhance your investment success and achieve financial independence. As you commit to disciplined investment practices and stay focused on your long-term financial goals, you position yourself for financial success through strategic investment.

There are three main types of investments, these are stock, bonds and cash and they are referred to as Asset Classes. These classes all have different levels of risk however, the rule is to always buy low and sell high while keeping the fees as low as possible. The range of companies you can invest in includes small local businesses, emerging markets as well as international stock run by multi-billion-pound corporations.

Graph of risk vs return

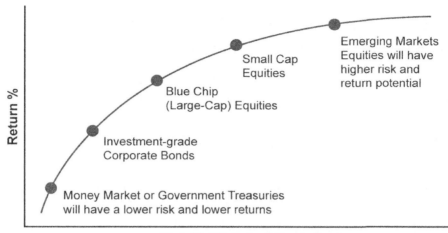

Stock

Ownership in a company classed as small, medium, or large where the company value determines the profits and losses. Stocks seek to provide long-term growth of capital by tracking the performance of the index.

Bonds

Bonds are a loan given to a government institution or a company and is repaid over a fixed period at a fixed interest rate. When the interest rate goes up, the value of the bond also increases and vice versa. The longer the bond term, the higher the risk and the shorter the bond, the lower the risk. Bonds provide returns consistent with the performance of the index.

Cash

Cash is the least risky form of investment even though it can depreciate and lose value over time. For example, a can of coke in the United Kingdom only cost £0.25 in 1997 but now costs £0.80 to £1 in 2019. And that means had I kept £0.25 under my mattress over the same period to spend it now, I would not be able to do due to inflation and other factors. Do not hide your money but put it to work.

Getting Started in Investments

The simplest way to get started in investments is to get someone to invest the funds for you at a fee and in line with your own capacity for risk. High risk investments give a higher return and lower risk investments will give you lower returns. Investigate every company before entrusting them with your money as they all have different types of charges. Some companies charge an exit fee for example, and you might be caught unaware should you decide to withdraw your funds. A wealth manager will typically charge about 2%, while a Robo advisor will charge around 1%. Most of the established companies are not the cheapest so you must compare to choose the best one for you. The alternative is to do it yourself, which works out cheaper though you must first get understanding, to get started by yourself. You will need to find a cheap platform charging around 0.2% in fees and buy cheap funds also around 0.2% in fees. A platform allows you to buy and sell, it also allows you to value check and provides you with the necessary research required to invest wisely.

10 Golden Rules of Investments

1. Investing in yourself is the number 1 golden rule in investments and you must always pay yourself first. Every time you get paid, never forget to pay yourself first before spending on anything else. Most people do not do this and by the time, they wish they had some money, other needs have taken precedence. You are the best investment that you will ever have, your time is priceless so educate yourself above anything else. Any business can be started and restarted but there is only one you in the entire world.

2. Invest monthly and invest long term. Develop the ability to hang in there and stick it out instead of jumping from one investment to another. Patience and stability are critical.

3. Get started by doing simple things such as creating a crisis or emergency fund for a 'rainy day.' Success is not an accident and does not happen overnight.

4. Make investment decisions based on the correct price and individual company potential and not on economic predictions. Research every company before investing and only invest in what you understand.

5. Do not invest out of fear or panic but always make investment decisions with a collected head. If in doubt or under pressure, sleep over it. But make sure that you do not allow the moment to pass you by.

6. Trade your cash for assets as money is always depreciating in value as mentioned in previous chapters.

7. Invest in income-producing assets such as a business or real estate. This is where your assets continue to bare more assets.

8. Do not trade your time for money and start moving towards residual or passive income. You do not have to quit your job right now but do not make your job your retirement plan if your desire is to become wealthy. Your goal should include moving from A – D or at the very least end up at C as Robert Kiyosaki demonstrates in his cashflow quadrant analysis:

    A. **Employees** – Work for someone else.
    B. **Self-employed** – Work for themselves.
    C. **Business Owners** – Have others work for them.
    D. **Investors** – Have money working for them.

9. Major on capital generation and never forget to always pay yourself first. This is the number one principle for getting rich. Make paying yourself automated, just to be sure.

10. Learn to diversify but always focus on specific investments until you succeed. The safest way to diversify is to invest in exchange traded or mutual funds that diversify for you so that your eggs are not all in one basket while someone else does all the juggling for you. This is also an opportunity to do some compounding by giving the instruction to have your dividends re-invested automatically for you instead of spending them.

And finally, change your thinking! Decide to get out of the box that has been created around you over the years. Most people have been conditioned to act and think a certain way and most of that thinking involves playing it safe and sticking to decisions that give you a sense of security. But the truth is that you can get out of containment; out of 'the box' and become a multi-millionaire in your lifetime, yes, it is possible, and you can.

UNDERSTANDING SAVINGS

49. UNDERSTANDING SAVINGS

Savings play a pivotal role in the creation of wealth, serving as the foundation upon which you can build your financial security and achieve your long-term financial goals. Whether it is setting aside funds for emergencies, investments, or future expenses, cultivating a habit of saving is essential for wealth accumulation. The number of people who have the bulk of their funds in current accounts that pay them absolutely no interest is astounding. Unlike in times past, today's banking systems and financial establishments offer much better interest rates for special savings accounts, which are available to anyone who qualifies to open a bank account. Ask yourself when the last time was that you looked around and compared the market for the best place to keep the bulk of your finances. In this chapter, we explore the significance of savings in the creation of wealth and strategies for maximising the impact of savings on financial success. Putting these strategies into practice can significantly change your life and set you on your way to success.

Establishing a Savings Mindset: Building wealth begins with adopting a savings mindset, which is a commitment to prioritising saving and investing a portion of income for future financial goals. You must recognise the importance of saving as a means of building financial security, achieving financial independence, and realising long-term aspirations. By cultivating a savings mindset, you can develop the discipline and habits necessary for effective wealth accumulation. A savings mindset includes having saving goals in place. Please follow the SMART goals system to do this.

Paying Yourself First: A fundamental principle of saving is paying yourself first by allocating a portion of income towards savings before covering expenses. This involves setting aside a predetermined percentage of income for savings and investments as soon as income is received, rather than saving whatever is left after expenses. By prioritising savings and treating it as a non-negotiable expense, you ensure that you consistently build your savings and progress towards your financial goals. Automating these payments is a sure way of making sure you never forget to pay yourself first.

Creating a Budget: Budgeting is a powerful tool for managing finances and maximising savings as already covered in the chapter we have just concluded. you should create a comprehensive budget that outlines income, expenses, and savings goals, allowing you to track spending, identify areas for cost-cutting, and allocate funds towards savings priorities. By adhering to a budget and monitoring spending habits, you can optimise their savings rate and accelerate wealth accumulation.

Automating Savings: Automating savings is an effective strategy for ensuring consistent saving habits and removing the temptation to spend funds earmarked for savings. You can set up automatic transfers from your current account to a designated savings or investment account on a recurring basis, such as monthly or fortnightly. By automating savings, you establish a disciplined savings routine and make saving a seamless part of your financial management process.

Prioritising Emergency Savings: Emergency savings are a critical component of financial security and wealth creation. You should prioritise building an emergency fund equivalent to three to six months' worth of living expenses to cover unexpected financial setbacks, such as job loss, medical expenses, or major home repairs. By establishing an emergency fund, you protect yourself from financial hardship and avoid derailing your long-term savings and investment goals. Chapter 17 above tells you more.

Maximising Savings Opportunities: Maximizing savings opportunities involves identifying ways to reduce expenses and increase income to boost savings potential. This may include cutting discretionary spending, negotiating bills and expenses, seeking discounts or promotions, and exploring additional income streams through side hustles or freelance work. By maximising savings opportunities, you can increase your savings rate and accelerate your journey towards financial success.

Savings are a cornerstone of wealth creation, providing you with the financial foundation to achieve your long-term goals and aspirations. By adopting a savings mindset, paying yourself first, creating a budget, automating savings, setting savings goals, prioritising emergency savings, and maximising savings opportunities, you can build your financial security and create wealth over time. As you commit to disciplined saving habits and prioritise building your savings, you lay the groundwork for achieving financial independence and realising their dreams.

THE POWER OF AUTHENTICITY

50. THE POWER OF AUTHENTICITY

Authenticity is a powerful force that influences every aspect of our lives, including our journey towards wealth creation. In a world filled with noise and distractions, authenticity stands out as a beacon of truth and integrity. In this chapter, we delve into the significance of authenticity in the creation of wealth and explore how aligning our actions and values with our authentic selves can lead to sustainable financial success. Authenticity is the quality of being genuine, honest, and true to oneself. It involves embracing our unique identity, values, and beliefs, and expressing them authentically in our actions and interactions with others. Authenticity is demonstrated in your transparency, sincerity, and congruent behaviour, which fosters trust and credibility in your relationships.

In the context of wealth creation, authenticity plays a crucial role in building trust and credibility with stakeholders, whether they are clients, customers, investors, or business partners. Authenticity enables you to establish genuine connections, foster meaningful relationships, and create value based on integrity and transparency. By aligning your financial endeavours with your authentic self, you can attract opportunities, resources, and success in your wealth creation journey.

Authentic wealth creation begins with aligning your financial goals and strategies with your personal values and beliefs. By identifying and prioritising what truly matters to you, whether it is family, community, integrity, or social impact, you can make intentional financial decisions that reflect your authentic self. This alignment fosters a sense of purpose and fulfilment in your wealth creation efforts, guiding you towards meaningful and sustainable success.

In entrepreneurship and business, authenticity is a powerful differentiator that sets brands apart in crowded markets. Authentic brands and businesses are built on a foundation of integrity, transparency, and genuine connection with customers. By staying true to your values and purpose, you can create an authentic brand that resonates with your target audience, foster loyalty, and drive sustainable growth and profitability.

Authentic leadership is characterised by genuine, empathetic, and values-driven leadership behaviour. Authentic leaders inspire trust, loyalty, and commitment among team members by leading with integrity and authenticity. As an authentic leader, you must embrace vulnerability, admit mistakes, and demonstrate humility, which fosters an environment of openness, collaboration, and innovation. Create a culture of authenticity within your organisation, driving employee engagement, productivity, and financial success.

In personal finance, authenticity guides you in making financial decisions that align with your values and long-term goals. By staying true to your authentic self, you can resist societal pressures and external influences that may lead to unsustainable spending habits or financial decisions that compromise your values. Authenticity empowers you to make financial choices that prioritise your well-being over materialistic pursuits.

Authenticity extends beyond financial transactions to encompass genuine, meaningful relationships with others. Building authentic relationships based on trust, respect, and mutual understanding is essential for creating a supportive network that fosters personal and professional growth. These relationships provide valuable opportunities for collaboration, mentorship, and knowledge-sharing, which are instrumental in driving wealth creation and success.

Authenticity is a powerful catalyst for wealth creation, guiding you and your business towards sustainable financial success. By embracing your authentic self, aligning your actions with your values, and fostering genuine connections with others, you create a solid foundation for building wealth and prosperity. As you navigate your wealth creation journey with authenticity and integrity, you not only achieve financial success but also cultivate a sense of purpose, and meaningful impact in your life.

THE POWER OF FOCUS

51. THE POWER OF FOCUS

Focus is critical for your financial success. In fact, broken focus is one of the greatest reasons for many failed dreams and ambitions. In the pursuit of wealth creation, focus emerges as a crucial element that separates successful people from the rest. By channelling energy, resources, and attention towards specific goals and priorities, you can unlock your potential and achieve significant financial success. In this chapter, we explore the profound impact of focus on wealth creation and strategies for harnessing its power to realise financial goals.

1. **Clarity of Vision:** Focus begins with clarity of vision, which is a deep understanding of your financial aspirations, goals, and priorities. you must define your vision for wealth creation, identifying specific objectives such as financial independence, asset accumulation, or entrepreneurship. A clear vision serves as a guiding beacon, enabling you to direct your efforts and resources towards achieving your desired financial outcomes.

2. **Setting Priorities:** Focus requires setting clear priorities and allocating resources. Your main resources are time, energy, and capital towards activities that align with your financial goals. By identifying high-impact tasks and projects that contribute directly to wealth creation, you can optimise your efforts and maximise returns on investment. Setting priorities ensures that you focus your attention on activities that yield the greatest financial rewards and long-term benefits.

3. **Eliminating Distractions:** Distractions pose a significant obstacle to focus and productivity in your pursuit of wealth. You must identify and eliminate distractions, whether they are external factors like social media, entertainment, or unproductive habits that divert attention from your financial goals. By creating a conducive environment for focus, you can minimise distractions and maintain concentration on your goals.

4. **Concentrated Effort:** Focus requires concentrated effort, which means committing your undivided attention and energy to tasks and projects related to wealth creation. You must dedicate focused blocks of time to work on income-generating activities, investment research, business development, or skill acquisition. By immersing yourself fully in these activities, you can achieve higher levels of productivity and effectiveness.

5. **Strategic Planning:** Focus is enhanced through strategic planning that involves a systematic approach to organising and prioritising tasks in alignment with your financial objectives. You should develop clear action plans, timelines, and milestones to guide your wealth creation efforts. Strategic planning allows you to break down complex goals into actionable steps, enabling you to make steady progress towards financial success.

6. **Resilience and Persistence:** Maintaining focus in wealth creation requires resilience and persistence in the face of challenges and setbacks. You must cultivate a resilient mindset, staying committed to your financial goals despite obstacles or temporary setbacks. Life and business will

always have difficulties, and that is just the way it is. By persevering through challenges and maintaining focus on long-term objectives, you can overcome adversity and achieve success in wealth creation.

7. **Continuous Learning and Improvement:** Focus is sustained through continuous learning and improvement, through investing in education, acquiring new skills, and staying updated on industry trends and market developments. You should prioritise personal and professional development, seeking opportunities to expand your knowledge and expertise in areas relevant to wealth creation. By staying informed and adaptable, you can adapt to changing circumstances and seize opportunities for your financial growth.

The power of focus is undeniable in the creation of wealth, enabling you to channel your energy, resources, and attention towards achieving financial success. By maintaining clarity of vision, setting priorities, eliminating distractions, concentrating effort, strategic planning, resilience, persistence, and continuous learning, you can harness the power of focus to realise your financial goals and aspirations. As you cultivate focus and discipline in your wealth creation endeavours, you unlock your potential for achieving lasting financial prosperity and success.

If you want to win every time, just make sure that you stay authentic and find your purpose, then stick to your own lane. Please do not go to the grave without discovering your purpose. Everyone in the scriptures who knew their purpose predicted their own end because they knew that they had fulfilled their reason for being and that includes Jesus and the Apostle Paul.

One of the greatest questions you can ever answer, is the question of your identity and purpose. It is only when you know where you are going that you will then be able to know exactly what roads to take to get there. There will be other roads along the way and attractive sights to turn into but when you are focused on your destination, these will do little to derail you and set you off course. Here are a few important things you must understand to be able to complete your journey successfully:

Understand who you are!

You cannot expect everyone else to understand you when you do not even understand yourself. The question of who you are is tied to your purpose in this life and not necessarily in what you do. Many people think they are what they do, however, your identity goes far beyond that. Every created entity is best designed by its creator and in your case, your identity can be traced back to God. When you discover who you truly are, success will follow by design, and you will not need to strive too hard. Consider a fish called Jack, who does not know who he is, so he is busy trying to swim on the road and things look bad. He cries out for help and complains about the road surface, he complains about the people and cars causing so much noise and chaos among other things. Then one day, someone comes to him and helps him understand that he is a fish and is designed to thrive in water. He realises who he is and jumps into the river, in that instant, his life is transformed from failure to great victory as he discovers that he flourishes nicely when operating in his own lane.

Knowing your path and sticking to your lane is non-negotiable, period. Nobody wants to spend a lifetime trying to be somebody else, a photocopy or worse still, a fake. That is why I always say that I will never be the next anybody because I can only be me. Being me is the best I will ever be able to achieve, as that is all the grace I have for my purpose. Part of understanding who you are is understand where you are coming from first and then linking that knowledge to where you are now. After which, you can then see where you are going next. When you have taken this journey of self-evaluation and discovery, you can then begin to appreciate and understand the fullness of your potential.

When your parents got together before you were born, millions of sperm cells swam out to meet one special egg. Your mother produced and lost different eggs over many years before the special egg that would make you showed up in that special month. So, when the moment came and suddenly, there were hundreds of millions of sperm swimming in competition for that one special egg and you were the winner. You cannot even begin to imagine the odds that it would be your special sperm that would be the one to win the race and make contact. After making contact, you still needed to be the right fit to break through and fuse with that special egg. You had won your first race; your first assignment; you won your first test and that makes you a born winner! Out of the half a billion sperm cells released on that day, God chose you. Do not ever let anyone make you feel inferior or less than just because you are different, you were designed to be different; designed to stand out; you were designed to be a misfit; one in half a billion; one of a kind, so learn to give yourself some love and celebrate yourself as you stick to your very own lane. Become the best version of yourself and I will see you at the top.

THE ART OF CONSISTENCY

52. THE ART OF CONSISTENCY

Consistency is the cornerstone of wealth creation and financial independence. It is the disciplined practice of taking regular, deliberate actions aligned with your financial goals over time. While the path to wealth may seem daunting, consistency transforms ambitious dreams into tangible realities. In this chapter, we explore the art of consistency and its profound impact on achieving financial success and independence. Consistency is the quality of being dependable, steady, and unwavering in behaviour, actions, or performance over time. It involves the disciplined practice of maintaining a particular standard, approach, or pattern of behaviour consistently, regardless of external circumstances or challenges.

In various contexts, consistency manifests as:

i. **Reliability:** Consistency implies being dependable and trustworthy, consistently delivering on promises, commitments, and obligations. It involves following through on tasks, meeting deadlines, and honouring agreements consistently.

ii. **Steadiness:** Consistency involves maintaining a stable and steady course of action or behaviour, without abrupt fluctuations or deviations. It reflects a sense of predictability and stability in one's actions, decisions, and responses.

iii. **Uniformity:** Consistency entails adhering to a standard or pattern of behaviour consistently across different situations or contexts. It involves maintaining coherence and conformity in actions, attitudes, and approaches over time.

iv. **Persistence:** Consistency embodies the perseverance and determination to continue pursuing goals or objectives steadfastly, even in the face of obstacles, setbacks, or challenges. It involves staying committed and focused on achieving desired outcomes over the long term.

v. **Repeatability:** Consistency involves producing the same results or outcomes consistently when repeating a task, process, or action under similar conditions. It reflects the ability to replicate successful outcomes through systematic and consistent execution.

Consistency is a fundamental trait associated with reliability, steadiness, uniformity, persistence, and repeatability in behaviour, actions, or performance. It is a key factor in achieving success, building trust, and fostering personal and professional growth. Here are a few keys that will help you master the art of consistency and win in your journey to financial freedom:

1. Building Strong Financial Habits:

Consistency begins with the cultivation of strong financial habits. Establishing a routine of saving, investing, and budgeting lays the foundation for long-term financial success. By consistently allocating a portion of your income towards savings and investments, you harness the power of compound interest to grow your wealth exponentially over time.

2. Setting Clear Financial Goals:

Consistency is fuelled by clear, well-defined financial goals. Whether it is saving for retirement, purchasing a home, or starting a business, setting specific, measurable goals provides direction and purpose to your financial journey. Consistently revisiting and refining these goals ensures that your actions remain aligned with your aspirations, driving you closer to financial independence.

3. Committing to Continuous Learning:

Consistency in wealth creation requires a commitment to continuous learning and self-improvement. Stay informed about financial markets, investment strategies, and economic trends through books, courses, seminars, and reputable financial resources. By consistently expanding your knowledge and staying abreast of industry developments, you empower yourself to make informed financial decisions and adapt to change.

4. Embracing Patience and Persistence:

Consistency is synonymous with patience and persistence. Wealth accumulation is a marathon, not a sprint. Embrace the journey with patience, understanding that meaningful progress takes time. Persist through inevitable challenges, setbacks, and market fluctuations, remaining steadfast in your commitment to your financial goals. Consistency in the face of adversity separates those who achieve financial independence from those who don't.

5. Automating Financial Processes:

Consistency is facilitated by automation. Leverage technology to automate financial processes such as savings contributions, bill payments, and investment transactions. By setting up automatic transfers and payments, you remove the temptation to deviate from your financial plan and ensure that your financial commitments are met consistently, regardless of external distractions. Set up Direct Debits and Standing Orders.

6. Cultivating a Positive Money Mindset:

Consistency is fuelled by a positive money mindset. Cultivate a mindset of abundance, gratitude, and financial empowerment. Visualize your financial goals, affirm your ability to achieve them, and embrace an abundance mentality that attracts wealth and opportunities into your life. Consistency in maintaining a positive money mindset strengthens your resolve and resilience on the path to financial independence.

7. Reviewing and Adjusting as Needed:

Consistency requires periodic review and adjustment of your financial plan. Regularly evaluate your progress towards your goals, identify areas for improvement, and make necessary adjustments to your strategies and behaviours. Consistency does not mean rigid adherence to a fixed plan but rather a willingness to adapt and evolve in pursuit of your financial aspirations.

In conclusion, the art of consistency is the linchpin of wealth creation and financial independence. By cultivating strong financial habits, setting clear goals, committing to continuous learning, embracing patience and persistence, automating financial processes, nurturing a positive money mindset, and reviewing and adjusting as needed, you harness the transformative power of consistency to realise your financial dreams. Consistency is not merely a virtue but a guiding principle that propels you towards lasting prosperity and financial freedom. Your character is defined by your consistency.

THE POWER OF ADAPTABILITY

53. THE POWER OF ADAPTABILITY

Adaptability is a fundamental trait that empowers you to navigate the ever-changing landscape of financial markets, economic conditions, and personal circumstances. In the pursuit of financial freedom, the ability to adapt to shifting circumstances, embrace change, and pivot strategies is essential for long-term success. In this chapter, we explore the profound impact of adaptability on the creation of financial freedom and strategies for cultivating this essential skill to thrive in the journey towards financial independence.

1. **Embracing Change:** Adaptability begins with embracing change as an inevitable part of the journey towards financial freedom. Economic conditions, market trends, and personal circumstances are constantly evolving, requiring you to adapt their strategies and approaches accordingly. By adopting a flexible mindset and welcoming change as an opportunity for growth and innovation, you can navigate uncertainties and capitalise on emerging opportunities for financial success.

2. **Agility in Decision-Making:** Adaptability entails agility in decision-making, responding quickly and decisively to changing circumstances and market dynamics. You must be able to assess new information, adjust your strategies, and make informed decisions in a timely manner. By cultivating a proactive and responsive approach to decision-making, you can capitalise on opportunities and mitigate risks in your pursuit of financial freedom.

3. **Flexibility in Strategies:** Adaptability requires flexibility in financial strategies, being open to exploring alternative approaches and adjusting tactics as needed to achieve financial goals. You should diversify your investment portfolio, explore different income streams, and remain open to new opportunities for wealth creation. By maintaining a diverse range of strategies and assets, you can adapt to changing market conditions and optimise your chances of achieving financial freedom.

4. **Resilience in Adversity:** Adaptability is underpinned by resilience and your ability to bounce back from setbacks, failures, and challenges on the path to financial freedom. You must cultivate a resilient mindset, viewing obstacles as temporary setbacks and learning opportunities rather than insurmountable barriers. By maintaining optimism, perseverance, and determination in the face of adversity, you can overcome challenges and stay on course towards financial independence.

5. **Continuous Learning and Improvement:** Adaptability involves continuous learning and improvement, remaining curious, open-minded, and committed to personal and professional development. You should prioritise education, stay updated on industry trends, and seek out opportunities to enhance your skills and knowledge in areas relevant to financial freedom. By investing in lifelong learning, you can stay ahead of the curve, adapt to evolving market dynamics, and position yourself for long-term financial success. The future belongs to those who can see it before it happens. Anticipate the future and equip yourself for it accordingly.

6. **Strategic Planning and Risk Management:** Adaptability requires strategic planning and risk management—anticipating potential challenges and proactively adjusting strategies to mitigate risks. You should conduct scenario planning, stress-test your financial plans, and have contingency plans in place to navigate unforeseen events. By incorporating flexibility and resilience into your financial planning process, you can adapt to changing circumstances and protect your path to financial freedom.

7. **Embracing Innovation and Creativity:** Adaptability involves embracing innovation and creativity, exploring latest ideas, technologies, and approaches to wealth creation. You should foster a culture of innovation, experiment with new strategies, and leverage emerging trends to stay ahead in your pursuit of financial freedom. By embracing a spirit of creativity and innovation, you can identify new opportunities, disrupt industries, and create sustainable sources of wealth.

The power of adaptability is undeniable in the creation of financial freedom, empowering you to thrive in the face of uncertainty and change. By embracing change, agility in decision-making, flexibility in strategies, resilience in adversity, continuous learning, strategic planning, and risk management, and embracing innovation and creativity, you can cultivate adaptability as a core skill in your journey towards financial independence. As you develop a mindset of adaptability and resilience, you unlock your potential to navigate challenges, seize opportunities, and achieve lasting financial freedom.

SWOT ANALYSIS

54. SWOT ANALYSIS

SWOT analysis, which stands for Strengths, Weaknesses, Opportunities, and Threats, can be a valuable tool in the pursuit of financial freedom. By conducting a SWOT analysis, you can gain a comprehensive understanding of your current financial situation, identify areas for improvement, and capitalise on opportunities to enhance your financial well-being. Let us explore how SWOT analysis can be applied in the context of achieving financial freedom:

1. **Strengths:**

    - Identify your financial strengths, such as stable income streams, valuable skills or expertise, strong savings habits, or assets with appreciating value.

    - Leverage your strengths to your advantage, whether it is maximising your income potential, using your skills for additional income streams, or leveraging assets for investment opportunities.

    - Recognise and capitalise on your unique strengths to build a solid foundation for achieving financial freedom. Your inherent gift is your superpower.

2. **Weaknesses:**

    - Assess your financial weaknesses, such as high levels of debt, low savings, lack of budgeting or financial planning, or limited knowledge about investment strategies. Assess your skill deficiencies.

- Develop strategies to address and overcome your weaknesses, whether it is creating a debt repayment plan, establishing a budget, improving financial literacy, or seeking professional guidance.
- By addressing your weaknesses proactively, you can mitigate potential obstacles and strengthen your financial position on the path to financial freedom.

3. **Opportunities:**
   - Identify potential opportunities for financial growth and advancement, such as career advancement, investment opportunities, entrepreneurial ventures, or favourable market conditions.
   - Evaluate the feasibility and potential returns of each opportunity and prioritise those that align with your financial goals and risk tolerance.
   - Seize opportunities to increase your income, grow your assets, and diversify your sources of wealth accumulation, accelerating your journey towards financial freedom.

4. **Threats:**
   - Anticipate potential threats to your financial freedom, such as economic downturns, job instability, unexpected expenses, inflation, or market volatility.
   - Develop contingency plans to mitigate threats and protect your financial well-being, such as building an emergency fund, securing insurance coverage,

- diversifying investments, or maintaining a conservative financial approach.

- By identifying and preparing for potential threats, you can safeguard your financial stability and resilience in the face of unforeseen challenges.

In Summary, conducting a SWOT analysis in the pursuit of financial freedom empowers you to assess your current financial situation, capitalise on strengths, address weaknesses, seize opportunities, and mitigate threats. By leveraging this strategic framework, you can develop a holistic and proactive approach to achieving financial freedom and building a secure financial future.

TRANSFORMATIONAL THINKING

55. TRANSFORMATIONAL THINKING

Transformational thinking is a mindset that transcends conventional boundaries, challenges limiting beliefs, and opens up new possibilities for wealth creation. By embracing innovative ideas, creative solutions, and visionary perspectives, you can transform your approach to wealth creation and unlock untapped potential. In this chapter, we explore the profound impact of transformational thinking on the creation of wealth and strategies for cultivating this mindset to achieve financial success. The process of rewiring neural pathways to transform your mindset towards financial increase involves leveraging the principles of neuroplasticity, which is the brain's ability to reorganise and form new neural connections throughout life in response to learning, experience, and environmental stimuli. By understanding the science behind neuroplasticity and applying targeted strategies, you can reshape your thought patterns, beliefs, and behaviours related to money and financial success. Here is how it works:

1. **Understanding Neuroplasticity:** As already discussed in chapter 3, Neuroplasticity refers to the brain's capacity to adapt and reorganise its structure and function in response to experiences, learning, and environmental stimuli. This process involves the formation of new neural connections also known as synaptic plasticity, and the pruning of existing connections based on the frequency and intensity of neural activity. Through neuroplasticity, the brain can rewire itself to optimise performance, learn new skills, and adapt to change.

2. **Identifying Limiting Beliefs and Thought Patterns:** The first step in rewiring neural pathways related to financial increase is identifying and challenging limiting beliefs and thought patterns that may be hindering progress. These beliefs, often formed during childhood or influenced by past experiences, can create mental barriers and negative self-talk surrounding money, success, and abundance. By bringing awareness to these beliefs and questioning their validity, you can begin to dismantle them and replace them with more empowering beliefs.

3. **Setting Clear Financial Goals:** Neuroplasticity is enhanced when you set clear, specific, and achievable financial goals. By defining their desired financial outcomes and breaking them down into actionable steps, you create a roadmap for success that guides their neural pathways toward the desired outcome. Regularly visualising and affirming these goals activates the brain's reward system, reinforcing positive neural pathways associated with increase.

4. **Practicing Visualisation and Affirmation Techniques:** Visualisation and affirmation techniques leverage the brain's ability to create mental representations of desired outcomes and reinforce positive beliefs. By vividly imagining yourself achieving your financial goals and repeating affirmations that reinforce abundance and prosperity, you activate neural pathways associated with success and abundance. Consistent practice of these techniques strengthens these neural connections over time, making them more ingrained and automatic.

5. **Exposure to Positive Financial Influences:** Surrounding yourself with positive financial influences, such as mentors, role models, and supportive communities, can also facilitate the rewiring of neural pathways related to financial increase. By observing and learning from people who have achieved financial success, you can model their behaviours and attitudes, reinforcing positive neural pathways associated with wealth creation and abundance.

6. **Consistent Repetition and Reinforcement:** Consistency is key to rewiring neural pathways effectively. By consistently engaging in activities that support financial growth, such as budgeting, investing, and seeking financial education, you strengthen the neural connections associated with these behaviours. Regular repetition and reinforcement of positive financial habits help solidify new neural pathways and override old, limiting ones.

7. **Shifting Paradigms:** Transformational thinking begins with a shift in paradigms, a departure from traditional modes of thinking and a willingness to explore new perspectives and ideas. You must challenge existing assumptions, beliefs, and limitations that may hinder your ability to create wealth. By embracing a growth mindset and questioning the status quo, you can unlock new pathways to success.

8. **Embracing Innovation:** Transformational thinking involves embracing innovation and creativity as catalysts for wealth creation. You should seek out innovative ideas, technologies, and business models that have the potential to disrupt industries and create value. By fostering a culture of innovation and experimentation, you can

identify new opportunities for wealth creation and differentiate themselves in competitive markets.

9. **Embracing Change:** Transformational thinking requires embracing change as a catalyst for growth and evolution in wealth creation endeavours. You should adopt a flexible and adaptive mindset, welcoming change as an opportunity to gain experience, grow, and innovate. By embracing uncertainty and proactively adapting to evolving market dynamics and consumer preferences, you can stay ahead of the curve and capitalise on emerging opportunities for wealth creation.

10. **Collaborative Partnerships:** Transformational thinking involves fostering collaborative partnerships and networks to amplify wealth creation efforts. You should seek out strategic alliances, partnerships, and mentorships that complement your strengths and provide access to resources, expertise, and opportunities. By leveraging collective intelligence and pooling resources, you can accelerate your wealth creation journey and achieve greater impact and success.

The power of transformational thinking is evident in its ability to revolutionise conventional approaches to wealth creation and unleash untapped potential for financial success. By shifting paradigms, embracing innovation, leading with vision, embracing change, cultivating resilience, fostering collaboration, and prioritising lifelong learning, you can harness the power of transformational thinking and unlock new possibilities, to achieve your financial goals and aspirations.

MY CONCLUDING THOUGHTS

56. MY CONCLUDING THOUGHTS

I hope you have enjoyed this journey with me and are ready to go after your dreams and live the life you really want, instead of the one handed to you by your circumstances whether current or past. If individuals in any society become wealthy, their nation will be better off, and the economy of that nation will become a thriving one. Having said that, there is no government or system that can keep you from prospering if you are determined and have resolved within yourself to succeed. Do not wait until everything is perfect but begin your journey to financial freedom today. Ask life the right questions and you will get the answers you seek. Become a student of wealth creation and diligently apply the knowledge that you acquire. Knowledge only works for you when you use it, just like you will die of starvation if you refuse to eat for a long time even though there may be food in your kitchen. Ignorance is extremely expensive, and many people are poor today because of it.

When you find your passion and discover what you wish to embark on, do it with everything within you, become obsessed with your vision and have faith in your vision. Study this book repeatedly until you have mastered it. Money Wisdom contains everything you need to know to be successful and become very wealthy. Never give up regardless of how difficult your journey gets, only you hold the power to all the keys that unlock wealth and riches. Change your thinking and change your environment, do not profess to know everything because if you did, you would be very wealthy by now. Some of you have already become rich and I congratulate you. Be sure to educate somebody else and pass on the knowledge and tools that made you successful. If you are still searching, I have good news for you: you can acquire everything you want in life by meeting other people's needs. There is no way you will solve a need in the world and not receive compensation for your effort. Become a solution to the world by identifying the key issues and challenges facing our world today. Once you have found a need and you have discovered a solution for it, get started and do not wait any longer. You are not in business until you are in business.

In conclusion, "Money Wisdom and The Laws that Govern Wealth" serves as a comprehensive guide to understanding the principles, strategies, and mindset necessary for achieving financial success and building lasting wealth. Throughout this book, we have explored the fundamental laws and principles that govern wealth creation, delving into topics such as the power of compounding, the law of supply and demand, the importance of delayed gratification, and the significance of financial literacy.

One of the key takeaways from this book is the recognition that wealth creation is not merely a matter of luck or circumstance, but rather a result of disciplined adherence to timeless principles and laws. By understanding and applying these principles in your financial endeavours, you empower yourself to take control of your financial destiny and work towards achieving your long-term goals. We have also emphasised the importance of developing a wealth mindset, an attitude characterised by intentionality, discipline, and a long-term perspective. Cultivating this mindset involves adopting habits such as living below or within your means, prioritising savings, and investments, and embracing a continuous learning mindset to stay informed about financial markets and opportunities.

Furthermore, this book underscores the significance of adaptability and resilience in the pursuit of financial freedom. In a rapidly changing world, the ability to adapt to shifting circumstances, embrace change, and pivot strategies is essential for long-term success. By fostering a mindset of adaptability and resilience, you can navigate challenges, seize opportunities, and achieve your financial goals. "Money Wisdom and The Laws that Govern Wealth" serves as a roadmap for individuals seeking to build lasting wealth and financial independence. By understanding and applying the principles and laws outlined in this book, readers can embark on a journey towards financial freedom, security, and prosperity. It is my hope that the insights and strategies shared in this book will empower readers to take control of their financial futures and unlock their full potential for wealth creation. Thank you for your attention and please be sure to pass this priceless knowledge on and empower somebody else.

ACKNOWLEDGEMENTS

57. ACKNOWLEDGEMENTS

*I**Am eternally grateful to God for giving me this amazing privilege of having the strength and perseverance to put this wonderful piece of work together, for the betterment of so many lives across the globe. I believe that this book will continue to touch and transform lives long after I am gone, and that has always been my drive and passion – to leave an indelible mark on my generation and generations to come. I am grateful to my family, my friends, my mentors, and coaches both past and present, including those who may never even know just how much they have contributed to my life through their words and their writings, thank you. To my wonderful editor, Georgina Isnes, only God knows how much you are appreciated and celebrated by me. May the LORD be your recompense and continue to bless and increase you more, may He bless the work of your hands and prosper everything that you touch. I would also like to thank my Grace Church Global family and the DK Global Foundation, for all your love and support always. The same goes for my DK Global Group family, thank you for taking this journey with me. I look forward to our best days together still to come as we soar higher and win together. This book has demanded more of me than any other book I have had the privilege to write so far, and I am much stronger for it.*

Printed in Great Britain
by Amazon